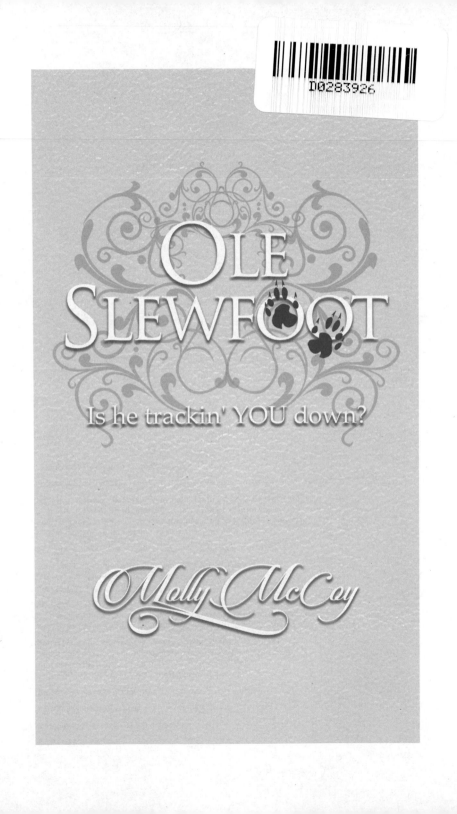

OLE SLEWFOOT

Is he trackin' YOU down?

Molly McCoy

Ole Slewfoot: Is he trackin' YOU down?

©2019 by Molly McCoy

Published by Carpenter's Son Publishing, Franklin, Tennessee

Published in association with Roaring Lambs Publishing and Larry Carpenter of Christian Book Services, LLC
www.christianbookservices.com

The Authorized (King James) Version of the Bible ('the KJV'), the rights in which are vested in the Crown in the United Kingdom, is reproduced here by permission of the Crown's patentee, Cambridge University Press.

Quotes by Adrian Rogers may not be reproduced or transmitted in any form or by any means — electronic, mechanical, photocopy, recording or any other — except for brief quotations, without prior permission from Love Worth Finding Ministries.

Cover and Interior Layout Design by Debbie Manning Sheppard

Edited by Christy Callahan

Printed in the United States of America

978-1-946889-92-8

OLE SLEWFOOT

Is he trackin' YOU down?

MOLLY MCCOY

DEDICATION

This book is dedicated to my Father in Heaven and His Eternal Kingdom. In Love, He has given me everything ... and in love, I owe Him everything. His Love, Mercy, and Grace have made this book possible.

This book is dedicated to God the Son – my Lord and Saviour, Jesus Christ. In Love, He has "Saved" me and "called" me to send this book out to His "called-out-ones." Those who read this book are "called" to do so (what they do with Jesus is their own personal choice).

This book is dedicated to God the Holy Spirit – our God Friend, our Good Friend. In Love, He witnesses to the spirits of the "Redeemed" that we are the Children of God. *And* He convicts and convinces the lost that they need to be. He is Jesus' dedicated hard Worker, and I dedicate this book to Him (and He will just give all the Glory to Jesus).

Therefore, so will I. This book is dedicated unto Jesus Christ Who Loves us and washed us from our sins in His own Blood and hath made us kings and priests unto God His Father – to *Him* be Glory, Praise, Honor, and Dominion forever and ever.

This book is dedicated to God's Holy Eternal Kingdom into which He graciously adopts us. We know that none of us are deserving of such Love and Mercy, but we *can* say "Thank

You!" Through the Supernatural Power of God the Father, God the Son, and God the Holy Spirit, may many more souls be added to God's Kingdom as His Holy Spirit speaks to their hearts through the words of this book. All Praise and Honor and Glory to our Great God – the God of All Creation! The God of our Salvation!

This book is dedicated to you, the reader. Read and be *Gloriously Saved*! Read and be *Gloriously Blessed* by The One Who is working *Mighty Miracles* in your life. May this book be a special Blessing from the Lord to His "called-out ones" – Whom He is using to build His Church in this generation.

My prayer is that this book will Eternally Glorify and Magnify our Great God. The souls who will be in Heaven because of this book will be to the Praise and Glory of God, and God alone. I thank my Lord for everyone who was a link in the chain of Christians who produced this book – all the way back to the Birth of our Lord's Church.

"SOLI DEO GLORIA!"

INTRODUCTION

M. A. G. A.!

My Friend, does your life have any meaning? *Serious meaning?* Yep, and whether you are not yet a Christian, *or* have been a Born-Again Christian for many years, you have just picked it up. The Lord is about to give *serious meaning* to your life. And don't tell me you're not interested. If The True and Living God didn't intend for your life to have meaning, He would never have put such a hunger for it in your soul.

God is very real, ever-present and fully "Alive" in America today, and He has an *Eternally* important "Meaning and Purpose" for *your* life. Starting today, God intends to use *you* to:

"MAKE AMERICA GODLY AGAIN!"

However, God's Plan is much bigger than just America. Now, I'm no Bible scholar, but in my humble opinion, I believe that God created this Universe and man upon Planet Earth for the purpose of defeating His arch-enemy, satan. Really! The Bible tells us of a time in Eternity past in Heaven when the Angel Lucifer rebelled and challenged God. That resulted in God needing a place of exile to which He could banish him. *So ...* God created the Universe, Planet Earth, and all things thereupon and called it *all* Good!

Then, God summoned His fallen angel and said, "Well, Lucifer, what do you think of *that?*"

Lucifer, with a sour look on his face, sneered and said, "Ugh, is that the best you can do, God? *I* could have done a much better job myself."

So, God responded in a thunderous voice, "OK, you devil, have at it!!" And with that, God kicked Lucifer out of Heaven in a lightning flash. He landed on Planet Earth, and today we have the world *satan* has created. God created Adam in His Image (the *Imago Dei*), and evil satan re-created Adam in *his* image.

(**NOTE:** I am convinced that mosquitoes were totally the devil's idea. And we know for sure that snakes were. That's reason enough to be agin satan right there. But it gets even worse. Every time you stand beside the casket of a loved-one, remember, *that* was satan's idea too.)

Now, you'll have to admit that the devil *has* done a great job of totally wrecking and destroying every good thing *God* ever created. *But* it ain't all over 'til the Lord Jesus says it's over. The last chapter of the Bible ends with God *defeating* satan … and *we* are all key players in God's strategy along the way. So, becoming a Christian is just the beginning of your "new Life" that has no ending!

"Behold, this is our God:
we have waited for Him, and He will 'Save' us!"

(ISAIAH 25:9).

This book is "Jesus" revealing His Great Love for you and His Big Plans for you as well. So, lift your eyes from whatever you may *think* your life here is all about and fix them solidly on God's "Real Reason" for sending you to Planet Earth. You are here on a Divinely designed Mission for Jesus Christ, God's Son – the Living Word! *But* Jesus can't use you until He first gets you onto His side and off of satan's side. And *that* is what *Ole Slewfoot* is all about.

Let me introduce myself. I'm an elderly servant of the Lord Jesus who has been sent out at this eleventh hour to serve at the pleasure of my King as a missionary ... to America, a very spiritually dark Country.

"These are the days when everything
that's not nailed down is coming loose,
and the devil is pulling nails as fast as he can!"
<hr>
(ADRIAN ROGERS).

"Lord God of Abraham, Isaac, and of Israel,
let it be known this day that Thou art God in Israel
(and America), and I am Thy servant,
and I have done all these things at Thy Word"
<hr>
(I KINGS 18:36).

Ole Slewfoot was originally the first chapter of my future book *Dare to Be Jesus* which was written to encourage Born-Again Christians to be strong Witnesses for our Lord and Saviour Jesus Christ. Yeah, I already know what you're thinking, "What?! I can't be *Jesus,* for pity's sake!!"

Well, think about it for a minute. If you are a Born-Again Christian, then Jesus "Lives" in you. So, you *can* let "Jesus in you" be "Jesus through you" ... can't you? If not, my book was written to inspire, encourage and help you live out your Christian Faith by doing *just that.* Now, I will admit, it *is* a radical concept. I'm a radical Christian. Jesus is a Radical Messiah. What can I say?

MOLLY MCCOY

*"I AM come to send Fire on the Earth;
and what will I, if it be already kindled?"*

SIGNED: JESUS (LUKE 12:49).

Now, I also know your next question, "How could just one chapter be soooo looooong!"

Well, I've been on the road to Heaven for lots of years, and I've witnessed to lots of folks. I've heard it all. So, I usually know what the unsaved are thinking. As I wrote, I tried not to miss anyone. However, as I kept writing, I managed to turn *Ole Slewfoot* into a "real bear." No doubt about it, I've got a lot to say and a little time to say it in. So, I want to make every day count ... for *Jesus*! That's why *Ole Slewfoot* has been turned loose in this world *all alone* to track down non-believers and bring them to the foot of Jesus' Cross so that He can "Save" them.

If that's you, then you were most likely given this book by a Christian who loves you and longs for you to be their Brother or Sister "in Christ." They are praying for you. I am praying for you. And last but not least, the Lord Jesus is praying for you. My prayer for you is that you will feel His tug on your heart as you read the message He has sent to you (through His servant) from the Throne of His Grace. It's time for you to be a part of "Something" *much bigger* than yourself. The Lord Jesus created you and purposed for you to be here *right now* ... so that He can have a dwelling place for Himself on this Earth. Interested?

The Presence of God is the most Powerful Force in the Universe! His Presence is with you as you read. My prayer is for this book to be a *very real* conversation between the Lord Jesus and *you*. Christ, and Christ alone, is able to burn the words on the page into your soul. Pray and ask Him to reveal His Truth to you. Ask Him if these are just the words of man, *or* if these are *"His Words."* The One Who Loves you *will* answer you.

So, don't be surprised when you feel the Lord's Presence and hear His still small Voice in your heart. And don't worry that He will show up and you'll miss Him. There's not a chance in the world that you will miss *God*. He will make sure of that. And when He asks you to trust Him ... *"Trust Him!"*

"Verily, verily, I say unto you,
he who heareth My Word and believeth
on Him Who sent Me, hath Everlasting Life!"
Signed: Jesus

(JOHN 5:24).

If you are already a Born-Again Christian, my prayer for you is that The Lord will use this book as a powerful "witnessing tool" in your hand ... enabling you to fulfill your Lord's Great Commission to you, because, sadly, the Great Commission is all too often the great omission.

When I was coming along, we had 'vagrancy laws,' and you weren't allowed to stand on the street corner holding a "Homeless" sign for very long before the police showed up and *gave you* a place to live ... for a while. Being a "bum" wasn't tolerated in the ole days, and our Heavenly Father doesn't want any bums in *His* Kingdom either. So, He is giving you a very meaningful job – as His Ambassador!

In case you haven't noticed, America is engaged in another Civil War. But it's not between the Republicans and the Democrats or the whites and the blacks. Nope, *satan* and his followers are waging war against God, His Son, His Word, His People, and the Christian values we hold so dear. I'm old enough to remember when America was indeed a Christian Nation, and I mourn the loss of my Godly Country.

Today, satan has won the war in our public schools and colleges where the liberals have taken over. Adults coming out of these schools are either atheists or worshipers of pagan "gods."

George Barna says that only 4 percent of our young people have a Christian world-view. America is morally imploding because she has destroyed her "Moral Foundation" by rejecting the True and Living God – Who loves her enough to die for her. And that's exactly what He did ... but America has forgotten.

My beloved America is being swept down a raging river of liberalism, humanism, atheism, and moral decay ... heading toward the waterfall of complete, unrepentant, total depravity. And the Lord Jesus is watching ... *you* – His Redeemed, Born-Again Child.

Only our Lord knows if we have passed that point in the river fearfully known as "the point of no return." But I know this, whether we have or whether we haven't, our Lord is still looking to His Children to do all we can to turn this Country around by paddling with all our might against this raging river. I can almost feel all the Heavenly Hosts watching and holding their breath as America hangs in the balance – at the edge of the falls!

Satan is the evil demon at the helm, and he's driving America over the edge of the falls into a spiritual darkness and death like we are only beginning to imagine. *So* ... will America continue on her path of ungodly, liberal insanity and go *over* the falls ... *or* come to her senses and *return* to the True and Living God, the God of the Bible? Our Nation can either fall on her knees before God, *or* He will bring her to her knees ... helpless before the Mighty God she rejected.

Every Christian *must* step up and start shining the Light of Jesus Christ into the dark souls all around them. *You* are America's only hope. If God's people fail in their God-ordained mission to America, the day *is* coming (you can mark my words) when the anti-God groups will be 100 percent successful in removing 100 percent of the mention of God from every building, wall, statue, and monument in Washington, D.C. (as well as every state, city, and hamlet in our Nation);

from every text book in public schools and from every public library! And when that happens, you can also remove the American Flag and replace it with the atheists' flag ... because America will no longer be the America God founded her to be. She will have failed Him the same way Israel did in days of old. If you are not a Christian, you laugh. If you *are* a Christian, you know it's so.

"It's really hard to have to watch
your Nation die on your watch"

(DAVID REAGAN).

America is standing at a "Mt. Carmel Moment." She must choose The God of the Bible, *or* choose to follow the "god of this world" ... to Judgment and disaster. As I look around, I see an affluent America – morally poor and spiritually needy before the God Who birthed her.

"Neither have we obeyed
the Voice of the Lord our God, to walk in His Laws"

(DANIEL 9-10).

But God is forever on His Throne, and *He* has a "Divine Plan" to *Save* America. He knows that she is sorely in need of myriads of Christian Missionaries – and He already has them here ... holding this book in their hand. *Mercy Me!*

When the Lord gets ahold of *all* us Christians, and we start actually getting His Gospel out to *all* those lost folks in *all* kinds of ways, *He* can win this war ... *through us*! If you aren't actively engaged in the battle, ole slewfoot has already knocked you out, and you're lying unconscious on the mat! Satan *thinks* you're down for the count. *But Jesus* knows that all you need is some of His Living Water to revive you. Open your eyes, jump up and get your second wind! The Holy Spirit is the Wind beneath our wings.

My Friend, this is spiritual warfare like I have never seen in my lifetime. You have doubtless heard of "standing your ground." Today, we Christians *must* "take back a lot of ground" stolen by our enemy, satan, while we were passed-out on the mat. We followers of Jesus need to quit retreating before bully satan and *his* followers. We must turn and let "Jesus in us" boldly proclaim, "Game On!"

> *"Life is too short ... Eternity is too long ...*
> *Souls are too precious, and the Gospel*
> *is too wonderful for us to sleep through it all!"*

(ADRIAN ROGERS).

Amen, Brother!

Those lost folks who need Jesus aren't going to be showing up at your Church any time soon. Nope, they aren't coming to Jesus. *Soooo ... you* must take Jesus to *them ...* right where they are – out livin' the high-life on the low-road to hell.

Young people are presently the larger part of our population, and they are mostly humanistic, hedonistic, non-religious liberals these days. They need to meet Jesus – Who is "Living" in *you*! So, "be Jesus" to them. Prayerfully give them the Gospel of "Salvation in Jesus Christ!" Jesus walked this Earth in Authority *over satan*. Today, He desires for you to *let Him Reign* once again in the midst of His enemies.

Now granted, you may feel like you're just the voice of one crying in the wilderness. *But* when you're lifting up *Jesus, He* will draw all men unto Himself! Jesus is The Light of the World. He is The Son ... we are the moon reflecting His Light and Glory to this dark, lost world.

> *"The woman at the well had a live-in lover.*
> *But Jesus knew she needed The Living Water!"*

(ALISTAIR BEGG).

OLE SLEWFOOT

She needed *JESUS* – the Healer of her heart, the Lover of her soul. And that's *exactly* what this lost world needs today.

"Hear me, O Lord, hear me, that this people
may know that Thou art the Lord God,
and that Thou hast turned their heart back again!"

(I KINGS 18:37).

These truly *are* the days of Elijah ... and you, my Christian Friend, are "Elijah!" There's no God like the Lord Jesus, and He is "Alive" in America today ... in *you*! *He* can give "Spiritual Life" to America ... through you!

Jesus is "Living" in *you,* Christian, and He wants to speak His "Message of Salvation" to the spiritually dead. Let Him!! Don't let satan silence you. No, the Church is a spiritual nuclear bomb just waiting to be ignited. Your deep, deep love for your Lord is the *Power* that ignites that explosion. When you let your love for Jesus overcome your fear, you will start telling folks everywhere about Him.

From sea to shining sea, America is shrouded in spiritual darkness. *But God* has *you* here for such a time as this. My Christian Friend, *you* hold the future of America in your hand ... because you know how to "Pray!" Pray for America and for the *Supernatural* determination *you* need to start letting Jesus flow out of you in a *Powerful* way to those lost folks you run into every day! If every Born-Again Christian would lead just one person to "Faith in Christ" this year, we would *double* our Christian population.

Let me tell you a Spiritual secret. Satan is shaking in his shoes (if he had any shoes) over the possibility that Jesus' "Soldiers of the Cross" will get their collective act together and start storming the very gates of hell. Everyday! Everywhere!

MOLLY MCCOY

"While we are waiting for Jesus to come down, Jesus is waiting for His Church to stand up!"

(SAMMY RODRIGUEZ).

Amen, Brother!

Now, I'm no Angel, but I have a message for you just the same: Ye men of America, why stand ye here gazing up into Heaven? This same Jesus Who was taken up from you into Heaven came back ten days later and is now "Living" His Life *again* in *you*! *And* His Heart is about to explode to tell *someone* (*lots* of "someones") that *He's here*!

Maybe you're a Christian who loves Jesus, and you really *want* to be His Faithful Witness ... *but* you're truthfully "the chicken of the sea." Well, don't worry ... help is on the way. Actually, you're holding it in your hand. Just give this book to a lost person and say, "May I share my Lord Jesus (or the Best News in the whole world) with you? Read this, and we'll talk about it later." If you give it to a total stranger you'll never see again, say, "May I share the Best News in the whole world with you? Read it, and talk to *Jesus* about it immediately!"

Now, I know what you're thinking, "It's not normal to just walk up to a total stranger and start talking about Jesus. It's just not natural." You're right. It's not natural – it's *Supernatural*! And only *Jesus* can do it. So, if you just don't love people enough to give them the Gospel of Jesus Christ, then let "Jesus in you" give it to them Himself. *He* Loves them enough to die for them. They are Eternal souls whom He deeply *Loves*. *This* is your chance to "be Jesus" to them. Go for it! Sure, it's going to cost you some time and money. *But Jesus* has all of Eternity to repay you. "Thank You, Lord!"

Only our Great God can "Save" our Great Nation. And He's going to do it through *you,* my Christian Friend ... *when* you walk up to people everywhere, offer them a Gospel tract and speak a few words about your Lord Jesus and His so Great Salvation. Just die to yourself and let *Jesus Live!* Hey, I do it all the time, and I promise you … it won't kill ya. In fact, it will make you more "Alive!" than you have ever been before in your whole life.

> *"Let the Redeemed of the Lord say so, whom*
> *He hath redeemed from the hand of the enemy (satan)"*
>
> (PSALM 107:2).

Now that the Lord has called Evangelist Billy Graham Home to Heaven, people are asking who the *next* Billy Graham is going to be. That's because they think that a Great Revival can only come through a famous evangelist. But the Lord has given me a very different vision – a vision of the next Great Christian Awakening coming to America, not just through one evangelist, but through thousands upon thousands of us Born-Again Christians out sharing Jesus with lost people as passionately as Billy did from the Crusade Pulpit.

So, who is going to be the next Billy Graham? *YOU* are. *Mercy Me!*

God's timing is always perfect. God took Billy Home to Heaven but left the God-given passion for sharing the Gospel with the lost that He had put into Billy's heart in *your* heart. In fact, just beneath the surface, the Lord has been slowly but surely *filling* your heart and soul with *that very same passion*! *Now,* God has placed this book into your hands. Could the Lord be trying to tell you something?

Today, Billy is talking with the Lord Face to face, and I can't help but wonder what they might be talking about. I have a funny feeling that they just may be talking about *you*! Now, I'm not saying that any *one person* will be the next Billy Graham. Not hardly. *All of us together* will be the next Billy Graham. And trust me, it will take all of us together to replace

Billy Graham. Can I get a witness?

"Amen!" (Thank you)

The only question is, "Will you trust the Lord to do it through *you*?" America will be great again when America is Godly again ... and you can be a part of this "Miracle in the making." If you believe, you will see *the Glory of God*!

In this book, I share some of my personal testimony of how my Lord "Saved" me. Before writing this book, I had never told anyone the details of my Salvation experience. I didn't want people thinking I was crazier than they already did. So, I went through life never sharing "my story."

However, in reading the Apostle Paul's accounts of *his* powerful Salvation experience, I have come to see that he certainly wasn't ashamed of it. In fact, he never missed an opportunity to tell people about it and brag on his Jesus.

So, I took a deep breath and decided to include some of *my* story in the book. And no, I did not see and hear the Lord Jesus with my physical eyes and ears. He graciously granted me *spiritual* eyes to see Him and *spiritual* ears to hear Him speak to me. And according to the Apostle Paul, God even gave me the *Faith* to believe! (Ephesians 2:8).

(**NOTE:** If it sounds like a "spiritual vision" to you, all I can say is that our Lord knows when He has a tough nut to crack, and He knows what it will take. But you may think that I was just delusional. To that, I will answer, "Whether I be delusional or not, I know not: one thing I *know*, that whereas I was blind, now I see! A Man called Jesus anointed mine eyes, and said unto me, 'Go!' ... and I went ... and I received. Thank You, Lord Jesus!")

If you aren't a Christian, then you have not yet experienced the *Supernatural Power* of God in Salvation. Let me reassure you that I and billions of other Christians (both on Earth and in Heaven) can testify (either in person or in writings) to the Truth of the fact that "JESUS *IS* ALIVE!" And His Gospel *is* the Power of God unto Salvation to all who believe!

Young Folks reading this may be a bit perplexed at times by the ole language, sayings and ideas presented in this book. That's because I was raised in an era before they were born. So, I draw my wisdom and words from a land before time. Well, *someone* has got to pass them on to the next generation, for pity's sake. Case in point: *Mercy Me!*

You've probably heard of the Christian band "MercyMe." Ever wondered how they got their name? Well, according to legend, Bart Millard (the lead singer) and his newly formed band were trying to come up with a good name for the group. One day they were all sitting around suggesting ideas and shooting down ideas until they were all out of ideas. Just then, Bart's phone rang. It was his Grandmother.

"Hey, Son, whatcha doing?"

"Hey, Grandma, the guys and I are just hanging out trying to come up with a good name for our new band."

"Well, *Mercy Me!* Why don't you get out and get yourself a *real* job!"

And the rest, as they say, is history (His Story).

So you see, us ole-timers *are* good for something. As you read, just remember you're listening to an ole-timer's voice, and you'll be fine. Now, we may not know an App from an Apple, *but* we do know this: When you belong to the Lord Jesus, He fixes you up and fills you up, then uses you up right down to your last breath on Earth. But there's more! *Then,* He raises you up in Glory, takes you up to Heaven, fills you up with His Joy, and Celebrates with you up and down Heaven ... *forever*. *Mercy Me!*

Us ole-timers know that we don't have much longer to spend dilly-dallying around down here on this Earth. No siree and a bob-tail bull, if we are ever going to do something for our Lord, it has got to be *now*! We know "it's now or never." We sense the urgency of the moment like no one else, and for us, the future truly is *now*. The time is short. Not only for us – but for *everyone*. Someone once asked Billy Graham what the most amazing thing he had discovered about life was. He replied, "The brevity of it ... how soon it's over."

You will see the words *but God* (or *but Jesus*) italicized throughout the book. That's because I believe they are two of the weightiest words in the Bible. How 'bout you? Do you remember when *your* life was a major mess, and you were dead in your trespasses and sins ... *but God* ... .!

This is my first attempt at writing. So, join me in praying for God's Anointing on this book.

"Nothing of Eternal significance
ever happens apart from Prayer"

(JERRY FALWELL).

Without God's Anointing, this is just another book. *But,* with *your prayers* and *God's Anointing,* He could use it to bring many into His Kingdom. God *knows* what He's about!

"Pray! Pray! Pray!" Ask our Lord to use *Ole Slewfoot* to defeat ole slewfoot! Then, use it to spread "The Great Christian Awakening" that is even now beginning to shake-up America! There is strength in numbers. The Bible says that one can chase a thousand. I wonder what a thousand could do. Let's pray and find out!

When we all become Soldiers of Jesus' Cross, we will "Make America Moral Again." This is a day of Good Tidings! Why sit we here until we die? Pastor Greg Laurie says that his job as a Pastor isn't his job ... it's "his Calling!" *This book* is "my Calling" to give *you* "a Calling" too. Use it to shine The Light of the Gospel of Jesus Christ into the dark souls all around you.

I am deeply indebted to one of my all-time favorite pastors, Adrian Rogers, whose insightful wisdom is included in my book. The Lord loaned him to us for a span of time, and now, has called him Home to Heaven to enjoy his Eternal Reward. For information on how you can be spiritually blessed by his preaching go to his website: **lwf.org** or call **800-274-5683.**

Tony Evans is another of our Lord's servants who has contributed greatly to His Eternal Kingdom ... and this book. You can find out more about Tony's Ministry at his website: **tonyevans.org.**

Ole slewfoot is hoping that no one reads this book (even though I named it after him). *But Jesus* has the last Word – not satan. So, I'm praying that this book makes it to satan's "banned books list" ... which will ensure that *everyone* will want to read it. Our Lord Jesus is well able to use man's "spirit of rebellion" to His own advantage.

Satan has managed to get a law passed in California banning books that speak out against the sin of homosexuality and transgenderism. OK, Christian Lawmakers in all other States, it's long overdue for *you* to pass a law banning all books that speak out against and attack the Bible, Christians and Christianity. Do only the *ungodly* get legal Constitutional protection these days?

Nobody ever apologizes to anyone for anything anymore, *but* we Christians are supposed to apologize every day to everybody for just being alive! America was founded on Christianity, the Bible, and Godly values, but today, satan's crowd has taken over. And Jesus' Followers are rolling over, playing dead and *letting them*. It seems that every group gets "special rights" and legal protection ... except Christians.

So Christian, don't let satan silence you any longer. The devil doesn't dictate to *me,* and Jesus can give you power over satan as well. Don't waste your time being afraid of satan. Instead, spend your time making sure *satan* is afraid of *you*! I'm pretty sure that my picture is on the bulletin board of the post office in hell. And yours can be too! God is just waiting for *someone* to stand up to satan. And when you do, He will honor your faith and courage – and *He* will stand with you. *Mercy Me!*

It is believed that the Apostle John was the youngest of Jesus' Apostles ... and he appears to have been the most courageous. Only John was recorded as being at the foot of Jesus' Cross at the crucifixion. There's just something about the young folks. They have the energy, zeal, boldness and willingness to be "all-in" and go "all-out" for that to which they have given their lives – Jesus and His Eternal Kingdom!

So, Christian Friend, join me in trusting our Great God to fill America's Vat with "New Wine" – a generation of *new Born-Again Christians*. We can only imagine what thousands upon thousands of "On-Fire-for-Jesus Born-Again Christians" could do in America today ... and for decades to come. Satan is absolutely no match for a bunch of energetic American teenagers set on "Fire" by Jesus Himself. Yes!

> *"Only a Nation led by God*
> *can lead the World!"*

(PETER MARSHALL).

OLE SLEWFOOT

"Blessed are they which are called
unto the Marriage Super of the Lamb."

(REVELATION 19:9)

Congratulations, my Friend! *YOU ARE CHOSEN*...to read this book. *Someone* put it into your hands – but *not* the one you think. The Lord of Heaven and Earth has a supreme purpose for *everything. He* is The One behind every "coincidence" of life.

Now, I know what you're thinking, "I don't believe that."

Well, why not wait until you finish reading this book to decide. *Someone* will make it very clear. He's the Master of making things clear. For instance, He said,

"All that The Father giveth Me
shall come to Me"

(JOHN 6:37).

This is the bold proclamation of none other than the only Son of God, Jesus Christ. Perhaps He was thinking of that moment in a wedding when the time comes for the father to walk the bride down the aisle and give her over to her waiting bridegroom.

So … has *your* time come? *You* think it's time for you to be entertained for a few moments. *But,* what if this unusual book fell into your hands because God has *'Willed'* it so … and *this* is your "Divine Appointment" with your future Bridegroom, Jesus Christ?

At this point, only the Lord knows. In time, *you* will know. By the time you finish this book, you will have answered the question: "What will *you* do with Jesus … Who is called *The Christ*?"

For now though, my Friend, you're still looking for a "quick fix" for your life … because you have written yourself off as a total failure. There are even those times when you think it might be a good idea for you to just "take missing" (otherwise known as *run away from it all*). But just remember: You have *one last* "failure" you haven't tried yet. You have failed to turn to the Lord Jesus, and *that* is the failure that has caused all the rest. *Mercy Me!*

In the South, we have an ole saying, "Honey Child, he ain't studyin' you."

Well, don't feel neglected, because I know of at least two persons who are studying *you* right now. One is the Lord Jesus and the other is satan himself. The devil is studying how he can take you down to the lowest level of hell you're willing to fall to. *But Jesus* already knows how *He* is going to take you up to the highest level of Heaven you're willing to ascend to.

"Verily, verily, I say unto you,
Hereafter ye shall

*see Heaven open, and the Angels of God ascending
and descending upon the Son of Man!"*

(JOHN 1:51).

Now, I know what you're thinking, "I don't see Jesus."

Yep, you're right. *You* live in satan's world ... where he has you blinded to the Radiant Beauty and Awesome Power of God's only Son, Jesus. But that's getting ready to change. Our Glorious Lord is more than able to break through satan's darkness and give you a Divinely *new* pair of glasses to wear – "Spiritual Glasses!" Interested?

If you are, you must first be confronted with some truths which will be foreign to your ears. For instance, no one has ever told you before that you are broken and need to be fixed.

Now, I know what you're thinking, "I was voted Miss Home-coming Queen. How could I possibly be broken?"

Easy. You're looking in the wrong mirror. You have never taken a look at your *soul*. *But Jesus* has shown up with His "Spiritual Mirror" to give you a good look at yourself ... and an even better look at *Him*. *Mercy Me!*

"There is none righteous, no, not one"

(ROMANS 3:10).

I once saw these words on the sign in front of a Church:

"FREE TRIP TO HEAVEN – INQUIRE WITHIN."

Now I'm making that same offer to you. Just keep on inquir-ing within the pages of this book, and you will learn how to ac-quire your own "free trip to Heaven!" It is God's good pleasure to reveal His Son to you – and He is your "Ticket" to Heaven.

You see, it's not *what* you know but *who* you know ... because who you know can tell you what you need to know ... when you know the right person – and *you do* ... because *now* you know *me*, and I can tell you everything you need to know about anything you ever wanted to know about Jesus ... because at this point, all you need to know is that you are a great sinner, *but Jesus* is an even greater Saviour – Who is lovingly reaching out to you right now through me by way of this *Jesus-sent* book. (Don't ask me to say that again ... just know that it's *true*!)

You don't know the Lord Jesus (yet), but you do know His messenger. That would be me by the way, and He has sent me to tell you that you don't need to be afraid of tomorrow. Nope. Someone Who *Loves* you infinitely more than you could ever imagine has your future all planned out. Yep, and He's got your Ticket *ready* for "The Glory Train" to Heaven. This is the day you hopped that Train ... because you can totally trust your Engineer. Step up, take your Ticket and get ready for the ride of your life!

"And the Lord God took the man ..."

(GENESIS 2:15).

God gave "Life" to Adam, and then ... *He took him.* The Miracle-working God Who created you has given *you* life, and *now,* He is ready to take *you* unto Himself. Are you ready? You will be ... when the Lord gets through giving you a good dose of *humility.* Before God can heal your soul, He has to humble your flesh. And having a little talk with Jesus – the King of Glory Who humbled Himself all the way to the Cross of Calvary to die for *you* – is a good place to start. Nothing frees you more than true humility.

OLE SLEWFOOT

God says in His Word that
"the unjust knoweth no shame"

(ZEPHANIAH 3:5).

(Hmmm).

Could that be you, my Friend? Do you refuse to look at your sin ... and blush? Instead, do you boast of that of which you ought to be ashamed? Well, you can either humble *yourself,* or *God* will humiliate you – big time ... in His time. God resists the proud, and no matter how hard you try or which way you turn, you will just meet with more of God's resistance.

"And thy heaven that is over thy head shall be brass,
and the earth that is under thee shall be iron"

(DEUTERONOMY 28:23).

"God is an expert at engineering our circumstances
so that we have nowhere to turn ... but to Him"

(CHARLES STANLEY).

There's one thing I know: The Lord of Glory has one thing on His Mind today – He wants to have a "Love Affair" with *you.* You've probably seen quite a few love affairs that ended with a broken heart, but *this* one *begins* with a broken heart – yours. The moment your heart breaks over your sin is the moment *this* Romance begins!

There is a Scared Romance deep within the heart of every man ... and woman. The desire God put into your heart for a lover is the Sacred Desire He put into you for an *intimate Relationship* with the Divine One Who brought you into being. Sex is a paltry foretaste of the totally exhilarating, completely satisfying union we shall have with the Lord Jesus in Heaven – *forever*! This book is "Jesus" bringing you into union with Himself – *now*!

MOLLY MCCOY

"By night on my bed I sought Him
Whom my soul loveth:
I sought Him, but I found Him not"

(SONG OF SOLOMON 3:1).

You have been trying to ignore the Lord Jesus all your life, *but* you cannot remain neutral concerning Jesus. You *must* deal with Him. You are either rejecting Him or receiving Him at this very moment. And trust me, He knows your heart. He *knows* which you are doing.

Maybe your life hasn't been going all that well so far. Good. God has you exactly where He wants you. Now you can cheer up ... because Jesus always saves the best for last. You'll see.

"The nine most terrifying words in the English language are:
I'm from the government, and I'm here to help"

(RONALD REAGAN).

Well, *I* have been sent from the Kingdom of God to tell you that *Jesus* is here! And He's here to help! Are you ready for some genuine help? The help the Lord Jesus gives you comes from *Another World* ... straight to your inner-world – the world of your *spirit*. The time has come for you to open your mind, open your heart and receive Jesus into your spirit.

So, don't let demonic pride keep you from Jesus. Don't let the devil trick you into believing that all you need is just a little religion, my Friend. Nope, what you need is a whole lot of *Jesus*! And not tomorrow either ... *today*! Jesus told the story once of a rich man who never showed mercy to a poor man on this Earth, but begged God for *His Mercy* when he ended up in hell – but it was too late (Luke 16:19-31). There is no joy, true happiness, or peace at the end of the road *you're* going down.

I know you. At this point in your life, you have decided that "the pursuit of happiness" is the all-consuming passion of your life. *But* what you don't know is that you never find happiness by pursuing it … because satan uses that which *you* use to "make yourself happy" to destroy you.

You think that pleasure, fun, and thrills are the ultimate achievements in life. That is satan's *ultimate deception* to keep you from seeking the truest pleasure and the greatest thrill in all of life – meeting and belonging to "The King of all Creation" – Jesus Christ!

> *"For God sent not His Son into the world*
> *to condemn the world, but that the world*
> *(including you) through Him might be "Saved!"*

(JOHN 3:17).

I know you. Deep in your soul, you're searching for … *something.* Well, good news! That which you have been searching for your whole life has finally found *you* … because you haven't been searching for *something*, you've been searching for "Someone" – and He's right here … right now.

> *"Doth not (God) see my way and count all my steps?"*

(JOB 31:4).

I know you. You just want some relief from all your troubles. *But God's* plan is to use your troubles to drive you to a "Divine Encounter" with His Son, Jesus Christ. God's ways aren't our ways – they are always way better. Your problems just aren't all that big … to God.

While you are running hard away from God, the Lord is running hard after *you.* And guess Who can run the fastest? So, you may as well just stop, turn around and cry out, "Lord! I surrender! I'm all yours. Take me and make me into the man You have always wanted me to be."

I know you. You're angry at … you don't know what you're angry at – you're just angry … because no one has ever answered any of your big questions in life – not the little ones like: Why does sour cream have an expiration date? – but the *big ones* like: Why am I here? How did I get here? Is there any purpose for my life? What's the meaning of all of this? Does anyone really care if I live or die? What happens to me when I die?

Now, I know what you're thinking, "You're right. I *am* angry … because no one is on my side. If I don't fight for what I want, I won't get what I want."

Not so. You forgot about satan. At this point, *he* is the evil one by your side, and that is why everything is always going sideways in your life. *But Jesus* has shown up to tell you that satan isn't the only game in town, and there's another team you can join … *Jesus' Team*!

> (**NOTE:** May I suggest to you that the *real* reason you're so angry is because unbeknownst to you (until now) you are one of the "condemned already" ones Jesus was talking about in John 3:18. *But,* when you become *accepted* in the Beloved Son of God, all of that will dramatically change. You'll see. At present, you will drink *anything*, take *anything*, wear *anything*, say *anything*, agree with *anything*, and do *anything* just to be accepted and loved by your "friends." But there is Someone watching you Who is infinitely more important than your friends, and *He Loves you* just the way you are … and He is just waiting for *you* to accept *Him*.)

I know you. You go through life afraid … of death. *But God* has arranged for you to meet His Son, the Lord of Life – *Eternal*

Life! The Lord Jesus is going to teach you that you don't have to go through life afraid to die, because when you belong to Him ... *you aren't going to*! Hallelujah!

On the other hand, you may be a person who doesn't spend much of your time thinking about dying. Before you finish reading this book, you'll understand why. So, I'm praying that you keep reading. That gives the Lord the chance to reveal to you the Truth: You're already dead. *Mercy Me!*

I know you. You desperately want peace in your life. You thought money would buy it for you. But now you know you were wrong. And *now*, you would give *anything* just to find some peace. Well, look all you want, my Friend, but the sad truth is that you won't find the true peace you're looking for in *this* world. Nope, it's in "Another World" ... where the Prince of Peace reigns in Majesty and Glory! The "good news" is that today He has decided to visit another world – *your* world.

> *"My Kingdom is not of this world!"*
> *Signed: Jesus*
>
> (JOHN 18:36).

There are places within you that you have never been ... because only the Lord Jesus can take you there. But Jesus can't take a dead spirit into a "Living World!" *So* ... He's going to have to do the same thing for you that He did for Lazarus – He's going to have to raise you from the dead ... because Jesus is *The Lord* of *the living*.

Now, you *think* you're *really livin'* at all those wild parties you go to, but that's just satan's slaves celebrating their master. If you want to *really live*, go to a Christ-centered Church and join in with Christians celebrating *their* Master! You can either celebrate Jesus or satan – you choose.

(**NOTE:** The way you feel "the morning after" will clue you in as to which is *the Right One.*)

We Christians are *The Picture of Dorian Gray* – in reverse. While Dorian's body stayed youthful and 'lookin' good,' his *soul* became monstrously hideous and loathsome (take note, those of you who embrace the sins of homosexuality and fornication). But, as a *Christian's* body ages and deteriorates, our *soul* grows closer and closer to our Lord as we reflect more and more of His Glory and Beauty!

Everything Dorian believed was fed to him by satan himself. Therefore, everything he did reflected the nature of his "master," satan. Everything we Christians believe is revealed to us by Jesus Himself. Therefore, everything we do reflects (or should reflect) the nature of *our* Master, Jesus.

Satan gets great devilish pleasure from defiling the pure and corrupting the innocent (like he did to Dorian), because misery loves company. *But Jesus* takes great pleasure in cleansing the defiled and bringing innocence back to the corrupted (like He will do for you), because *He* loves the pleasure of *your* company.

At the end of the ole 1945 movie, Dorian cried out to God for forgiveness as he lay dying of a mortal wound – the result of his sinful life. Now, it's wonderful to get to go to Heaven (even from your deathbed), but what a wasted life. God could have used your life to bring *others* into His Kingdom and earn *you* Eternal Rewards in Heaven. Don't get suckered-in by loser satan and his demonic temptations. "It jest ain't worth it."

Homosexuals who love Wilde's book just don't "get it." It is the worst condemnation of the homosexual lifestyle ever presented – and presented by the homosexual *himself*, for pity's sake! And *that* is what makes it so profound, because only a person who has lived the life can tell us the honest truth about it. Enter Oscar Wilde – the hero of every homosexual ... until now ... when the truth comes out of how he actually ratted on them.

The clear message of Wilde's book is shockingly simple: Give yourself and your body over to satan, and he will totally destroy your soul. Just ask Oscar Wilde. *The Picture of Dorian Gray* portrays the life of a homosexual as a living death. Dorian had "mad hungers that grew more ravenous as he fed them" ... and so did Oscar Wilde. Even though he knew what was happening to him, he was powerless to control it ... because satan had convinced him to lust after "eternal youth, infinite passion, pleasure subtle and secret, wild joys, and wilder sins."

So, why don't they "get it"? Why can't they "see it"? Perhaps, it's because they have long since nailed their soul to the devil's altar and left it there ... without any fear of the terrible consequences awaiting them in the future. Their temporal sexual pleasures are far more important to them than any Eternal pleasures in Heaven. They are "paying to play" using *a very valuable commodity* (their soul) which is being totally corrupted ... and they don't care. They have forgotten that the body they've forfeited their soul for is going to die one day ... and what then?

I'll tell you what then. *Then*, they will face all of Eternity with only their corrupted, satan-controlled soul left. Ole slewfoot is playing them for an Eternal fool, but he has them so spiritually blinded that they can't see it ... now. What an eye-opener their death will be! When they die and stand before King Jesus in Judgment for the life He gave them to live on this Earth, they will finally realize that sex is a mortal god, and that which they had made the god of *their* life is now gone ... *forever* ... and they will be so ashamed – but it will be too late.

Yep, *now* they are standing before the *True God* of this Universe — the One they *should* have been listening to all along. *Now* they will be forced to listen to Him as He says to them,

> *"I never knew you. Depart from Me,*
> *you who practice lawlessness!"*
>
> ———————
> (MATTHEW 7:23).

Was it worth it? They may be saying "yes" *now*, but I guarantee you … they will definitely be saying "no" *then*.

Now, I may not be the sharpest tack in the box, but even I can figure out the most *Eternally* wise thing to do here. And I'm praying that the Lord is sharpening up your spiritual vision and resolve too. Take my advice and go to the Judgment Seat of Christ *now* … then live your life backwards. What you want King Jesus to say to you on *that day* will determine what you do on *this day*.

Dorian Gray immersed himself in a sensual, sinful lifestyle, and he became evil to the core — like many in our world today. Just take a look around. They need to stop and take a long hard look at the monstrous, demonized *soul* Dorian possessed — and possessed *him* — after spending his life completely given over to sin and satan.

We humans are no match for evil satan and his strong magnetic pull toward sin of every kind. *But Jesus* in us Christians is stronger than he who is in the world. And even though we may sometimes have thoughts that make us *feel* as if we're as evil to the core as Dorian was … not so … because we Christians have *the Lord Jesus* in our spirits and souls *spanking* us to the core *and cleansing* us to the core when we have those evil thoughts. "Thank You, Lord!"

God, prayer, and the Bible are mentioned occasionally in

the book, but Dorian quickly and off-handedly rejects them ... deciding to follow satan and his wickedness instead. And such was the life of Oscar Wilde. In *his* day, the rulers of England still feared God enough to obey His Word; therefore, the sin of homosexuality was illegal. Nevertheless, Wilde flaunted his homosexuality before England's laws until he was eventually sent to prison. When he was released from prison, it was hoped by friends and family that he would return to his wife and family ... but he returned to his homosexual lover instead.

Wilde looked at life through the eyes of satan. *But Jesus laughs at the wisdom of this world ... it is foolishness to Him. True Wisdom is found in Christ, and Christ alone.*

The Lord Jesus stood before Oscar Wilde his entire life ... offering him forgiveness and Eternal Life (just as the Lord is standing before *you* right now offering you the same). But Wilde spurned the Lord Jesus his entire life. And then, came that fateful day when Oscar Wilde had to stand before the Lord Jesus. *Mercy Me!*

> *"For what shall it profit a man*
> *if he gain the whole world and lose his own soul?"*
> *From the lips of the Lord Jesus*
>
> ---
> (MARK 8:36).

Oscar Wilde died in infamy at the age of forty-six ... with his homosexual lover at his bedside. *The Picture of Dorian Gray* was quite autobiographical, and Wilde *knew beyond a doubt* that the picture of Dorian Gray was indeed the picture of *his very own soul.*

Where is he today? Where will *you* be after the Grim Reaper comes for *you*? You don't have to stand before God in judgment for Oscar Wilde ... only for yourself.

My closing argument is this: Give yourself and your body over to satan, and he will totally and devastatingly destroy your soul … as only he can do. When sex becomes your "god," you belong to a god that demands constant worship and complete obedience. Sex becomes sex for sex's sake, and apart from God's "Divine Design" for sex – marriage between a man and a woman – it is devoid of God's Love. You're just celebrating lustful sex instead of celebrating "The God" Who gives sex to *husbands and wives*.

So, call it what you may, *God* isn't in it … which probably suits you just fine, because God is the last Person in the world you want to run into right now. But since when have you ever stopped God from doing what *He* wants to do? And unbeknownst to you, God has just run into *you*. *Mercy Me!*

Only us older folks remember who used to sing out, ***"Here I come to save the day!"*** as he swooshed down in a blaze of glory to rescue some helpless victim from the claws, jaws, and grasp of some evil "bad guy." Yep, it was Mighty Mouse, and some things never change, because once again a Super Hero is swooshing down from the heights of Glory to rescue you from the grasp of evil satan. Yes siree, when there's a wrong to right, Mighty Jesus will join the fight!

The Lord has shown up with Good News! He has another message for anyone who has ears to hear: Give yourself and your heart over to the Lord Jesus, and *He* will totally and delightfully deliver you from the clutches of satan by "Redeeming" your soul … as only *He* can do. Then, your spirit, soul, and life will be full to overflowing with God's Love!

(**NOTE:** The "soul-life" is much more passionate and exciting that the flesh-life ever thought about being. You cheat yourself out of the deepest, most satisfying pleasures of life when you only live to satisfy the

> lusts of your flesh. I guarantee you that in the not-
> too-distant future you won't even remember many
> of those lovers you're sleeping around with now
> ... *but* you will never forget a person you truly and
> deeply love in your heart. And trust me, someone
> worth deeply loving isn't sleeping around with
> whatever "available bodies" they can find to use for
> a few fleeting moments to get a few immoral thrills.)

I once saw a sign in front of a liquor store which read: Be Always Celebrating! My first thought was, "What do they have to celebrate?" But, after thinking about it, I decided that *that* is the best advice we can give to those who *resolutely refuse* Jesus' Divine Invitation to come and join Him in *His* Kingdom. They need to celebrate hard on this Earth ... because it's the only celebrating they will ever do.

It is shocking to see how far and how fast England and America have fallen. Both Nations have radically changed their laws, but I can guarantee you this: *God's* Laws haven't changed, because God hasn't changed ... and He's watching it all (Malachi 3:6).

Satan absolutely loves it when he can get people to go *his* way instead of God's Way. The devil delights in getting people and nations to flaunt their sin openly and unashamedly before the True and Living God ... because that's the way he finally gets what he has always wanted – he gets people worshiping *him* instead of God. *Mercy Me!*

However, there is one thing satan can't do. He can't keep the clock from ticking. Yep, Mighty Jesus has a date with ole slewfoot. The devil believes in the Lord alright – and deep within his wretched self ... *he is trembling*.

Now, what about you? Do you love your sinful life more than you love the Lord? At this point, you probably do ... because you don't know Him yet. But He knows *you*, and He is drawing you unto Himself – a Saviour Whom to know is to love.

Now, before you throw this book aside thinking that I'm going to be speaking to you from some "Holy Pedestal" ... don't. I don't have everything all together in my life either. And at my age, even if I did, I certainly wouldn't remember where I put it. So, let me assure you that I'm a mess too, but at least I'm *The Lord's* mess.

So, whose mess are you? I'll tell you. The question posed on the cover of this book asks, "Is ole slewfoot trackin' *YOU* down?" Truth is, if you aren't a Born-Again Christian, the answer is, "No – he already has you." *Mercy Me!*

So, you're satan's mess. And his self-improvement plans don't work ... for very long. *But* you don't *have to* remain the dismal property of the junk-man of the Universe (even though he is frantically passing laws all over the world to prohibit Christians like me from rescuing helpless victims like you from his evil clutches), because I'm breaking his demonic laws in order to give The LORD of the Universe the opportunity to break satan's chains he has on you. It's D-Day (Deliverance Day) for you! The moment has come for you to sign *your* John Hancock to your own Declaration of Independence ... from satan.

> *"If The Son therefore shall make you free,*
> *ye shall be fee indeed!"*
> Signed: Jesus
> _____
> (JOHN 8:36).

The Voice of our Great God is going to be speaking to you as you read ... and you will have a choice. You can listen to Him, *or* you can choose to ignore His Voice the same way you have been doing *all your life.* The Good Shepherd wants to get you safely Home. *But you have to listen to His Voice.* The One Who *Loves* you more than anyone else on Earth wants to make you His own. You can keep resisting Him ... *or* you can yield to Him.

"Verily, verily, I say unto you, The hour is coming, and now is, when the dead shall hear the Voice of the Son of God; and they that hear shall live!"
Signed: Jesus

(JOHN 5:25).

So, just keep reading, keep pondering and keep your heart open to a life-changing encounter with the Lover of your soul, Jesus Christ. The very air you are breathing at this moment is a gift from Him to you. Unseen as air ... He is there. *HE IS THERE!* The Lord Jesus is *ALIVE!* And He wants to be *ALIVE* in *you!*

Jesus doesn't care if you graduated from Harvard, Yale, *and* Princeton with more framed Ph.D.'s than you have room on your wall to hang; He knows that if you don't have a freely given P.H.D.L. (Powerful Heavenly Divine Life) from *Him,* you're as empty as your wallet after taking your teenager shopping for a new pair of sneakers.

So, take a tip from one of Jesus' little Lambs, and take your very first step of Faith: Accept His *very real Presence* with you with every beat of your heart and every breath you take. As you draw near to *Him,* He draws near to *you.* The Glory of God has surrounded you your entire life ... without you realizing it – until *now!*

"I will send My messenger,
who will prepare the way before Me.

Then suddenly the Lord you are seeking
will come to His Temple; the messenger of the Covenant,
whom you desire will come, says The LORD Almighty"

(MALACHI 3:1).

My prayer for you is that the Lord will gloriously and suddenly come into *your* temple and "Save" you as you reverently read His Message to you. And when He does, He will translate you into His Heavenly World of "Jesus in you and you in Jesus!" If that sounds like a mystery to you, don't worry ... it *is* a mystery – a "Divine Mystery." And I want to be the spiritual Sherlock Holmes who shows you "The Way" into Jesus' World.

"The Eternal God is thy Refuge,
and underneath are the Everlasting Arms"

(DEUTERONOMY 33:27).

Even though you aren't yet a Born-Again Christian, you still have a tremendous power within you. It's called "the power of choice," and as you read, you can choose to *let* the Spirit of Christ free your mind from it's bondage to always thinking only on the physical level. Christ's Spirit frees your mind so that He can also free *your spirit* from satan's death-grip. With your spirit united with Christ's Spirit, you are then able to enter into the Mind of God and *His* Spiritual World. There you will get a glimpse of the mysteries of the height and depth and width and breadth of our Great God, *and* that you are "One" with Him. You are an Eternal Being created by God for an Eternal World! God has you "on assignment" here for a span of time ... *His* time. This is your "wake-up call" from the God Who created you. So, my Friend, wake up!

Those new-fangled computers nowadays have a button called the "Undo button." Many a time, that little button has saved the day when the nut in front of the screen has made a major mess-up. How many times have you wished *life* had an *Undo button*? If you're like me ... many times. Well, I'm going to introduce you to Someone Who has *The Master Undo Button*. It's called "The Precious Blood of Jesus Christ," and by the time you finish this book, you will know exactly how it works.

> *"Ho, everyone that thirsteth, come ye to the waters*
> *(Living Waters!), and he that hath no money:*
> *Come ye, buy and eat; yea, come,*
> *buy wine and milk without money and without price"*
> *(Jesus has already paid the Price on the Cross of Calvary!)*
>
> (ISAIAH 55:1).

By now, you've figured out who ole slewfoot is, but you can't figure out the Lord Jesus. That's because you have never had an encounter with Him of the Supernatural, Divine kind. Therefore, *you* are the number-one person the Lord wants to read this book. Really! Since you aren't yet a Christian, I wrote this book just for *you*.

And I know what you're thinking, "Why would anyone go to so much trouble and expense to write and publish a book for someone they don't even know?"

Answer: Because I know The One Who *does* know you. I also know that *He Loves you* enough to come to this Earth and die on a Cross to "Save" your Eternal soul! How can I *not* sacrifice myself for you? You need the Lord's Supernatural Power to reach out to you through the words on the pages of this book more than anyone else ... because Jesus says, "Ye *must* be Born-Again!"

However, if you have made up your mind that you have absolutely no interest in having an encounter with Jesus Christ and becoming a *Born-Again Christian*, you may as well just put it down now ... because nothing else I have written will be of any interest to you. Don't waste your time reading about "a Life" lived in "a World" that you will *never* be a part of ... by your own choosing. Just throw it aside and forget you ever picked it up.

(Wait ... wait ... wait ...)

You're still reading. Does that mean that you would *like* to have a "New Life" from the inside out?

OK, good. Here's how you can.

First, I need to ask you a question: Where were *you* when the lights went out?

Answer: You were in the delivery room being born!

The Light of the World is the Lord Jesus, and He was woefully missing from your spirit at the moment of your birth. Actually, it all happened a long time before that. Circumstances beyond your control caused you to be a "spiritual still-born." How do I know? Two ways.

First, God tells us in His Holy Word, the Bible, that *He Created* the Heavens, the Earth, and the first man and woman, Adam and Eve (the woe of man), to live on this Earth in perfect harmony and fellowship with Him.

(OK, Ladies, just kidding about us being the woe of man. We know that God took Adam's rib from him in order to fashion Eve *for* him. Therefore, Adam was missing a part of himself that only Eve could fill. Men don't like to admit it, but they know that we are God's precious gift to them to fill up what is missing in their lives. Right, Gentlemen?)

So, with Adam and Eve bonded together, God Reigned upon His Heavenly Throne and in the hearts of His Spirit-filled couple. All was well in His Glorious World ... until ... along came Lucifer, the fallen angel, to cause trouble in Paradise.

Let's pause for a moment and deal with the elephant in the room. Since you aren't yet a Christian, you believe in evolution. I deal with satan's evil lie of evolution in the chapter of a future book *Dare to Be Jesus II* entitled "A Monkey's Uncle." However, this book is mainly concerned with the battle between Almighty God and devious satan for your soul. So, let's choose our battles wisely and deal with your most pressing problem — satan.

Satan is your biggest problem because when you belong to him, he turns *you* into your biggest problem. Yep, and as long as ole slewfoot can keep you thinking that you are just an evolved animal, he can keep you blinded to who you *really* are: "A Glorious Creation" of the Miracle-working Creator God Who Loves you and has marvelous plans for you on this Earth *and* for all Eternity! You are *more* than a mere body. You, my Friend, are a *spirit-man* presently cut-off from the God Who created you. *But God* has put this spiritual-breath-of-fresh-air book into your hand to reconcile you to the Lord of Life. Yes!

Satan, on the other hand, is just a problem going somewhere to happen. Whenever ole slewfoot is creeping around, there's a bad moon on the rise, and whatever you have of value in "The Stock Market of Life" is about to go down ... down ... down. With the devil as your friend, you don't need an enemy — you already have the best fiend in the whole world.

"If you were sinking in quicksand, satan would pat you on the head and tell you that you're doing just fine"

(ADRIAN ROGERS).

So, that ole serpent slithered up to Eve and somehow persuaded her to obey *him* rather than God. (And no, I don't think she was blonde; however, I *do* wonder why she would waste her time listening to a talking snake, for pity's sake. But I can't throw stones at *her*, I do the same thing myself sometimes.)

Anyway, that smooth-talking, shifty serpent "spoke with forked-tongue" and promised Eve that if she would just listen to *him* and eat that fruit, *she* would be "as God." So, sweet Eve swallowed the devil's lies … as well as the forbidden fruit. "Adam's rib … satan's fib … women's lib!" (Adrian Rogers). Then, she gave some to Adam and became the first woman on Earth to bring a good man down.

Satan said, "You're going UP … UP … UP!" But instead, they went down … down … down.

At the moment of their sin, they died … just like God had told them they would. Really! They died immediately *in their spirit* because God immediately took His Holy Spirit from them … which caused them to die *progressively* in their soul and *ultimately* in their body. God is a Triune God, and you are a triune person – spirit, soul, body. And at *this very moment,* you are in the same desperate condition as Adam and Eve were at *that moment.* The devil's diabolical lie is still bearing fruit today – the lost condition of all mankind at the moment of birth. *Mercy Me!*

When Adam and Eve obeyed satan, they switched "gods" and allowed *the spirit of evil* to enter into their soul. The God (god) you obey is the God (god) you belong to. They chose to believe the lies of satan, rather than trust the Truth of the God Who created them. And you, my Friend, are still doing the same thing today.

Adam and Eve broke Covenant with God, and God broke

Fellowship with them. With the entrance of the devil's demonic power into their souls, God departed their spirits. And when God went out, the Light went out with Him. The "Life" of God's Spirit was withdrawn, and they were left "spiritually dead" in their inner-man.

The same wickedness that caused satan's fall now entered Adam and Eve and caused *their* fall. No more walking and talking with God in the sweet Fellowship of The Spirit. *Their* spirits were now dark and dead – separated from God. And when your spirit is separated from the Life-giving Spirit of God, death breeds like a canker in your soul! Everything you touch is left with the scent of death.

"And this is the condemnation,
that Light is come into the world,
and men loved darkness rather than Light,
because their deeds were evil"

(JOHN 3:19).

That was the most expensive piece of fruit ever purchased. Adam and Eve paid dearly. They exchanged the Life of God for the darkness and death of satan. It cost them the Divine Blessing of being "Spiritually Alive" in union with their Creator – the God of All Creation – the God of our Salvation! They went from standing on The Rock to hitting the rocks in a moment of time.

So, what happened? God "invited them to leave" His Holy Garden and probably said something like, "OK, Kids, since you have willfully chosen to follow satan, then just go on out there and follow him ... and see how you like it."

So, they did ... and they didn't. But it was too late. We make our choices, and then our choices turn around and make *us*. Sadly, *their* choice had made *them* "The Walking Dead!" *Mercy Me!*

However, since they were still physically alive, they had children ... just like their own miserable selves, who had children just like their own miserable selves, who had children just like their own miserable selves ... right down to *you*.

> *"Wherefore, as by one man sin entered into the world,*
> *and death by sin; and so death passed upon all men,*
> *for that all have sinned"*
>
> (ROMANS 5:12).

Your biggest problem in life is one you don't even know you have. "The spirit of the age" is *the spirit of satan,* because *he* controls every soul that comes into this world ... without their knowing it. And apart from the Divine intervention of God, we are *all* potential serial killers! Until you let the Lord "Redeem" you ... you're on death row. *Mercy Me!*

So, you showed up on Planet Earth physically alive — but spiritually dead. And you didn't even know it ... until now. Yep, because of sin, the only thing necessary for a person to be lost and on their way to "the place of Eternal death" is to just show up on Planet Earth. It's true, you were born lost — separated from God. As Tony Evans would say, you came here seriously "jacked-up!" And even though you looked like a sweet little angel, trust me, you belonged to the devil. There is none that doeth good ... no not one. If you doubt me, just ask the mother of a three-year-old if we are all born innocent little angels.

Nope, we're all born separated from God with neither the desire nor the power to love Him or please Him. Eve swallowed satan's lie — along with the fruit of it — and *now*, we (her Children) think that *we* are "god" ... therefore, everyone else needs to love and serve *us.* Sadly, instead of becoming like God, we have actually become like satan. You see, that ole devil is *still* trying to be God today – *through us. Mercy Me!*

Now, I know what you're thinking, "Well then ... if I'm a sinner by birth and a sinner by nature, I can't help but sin, right?"

That's right. As satan's slave, you can't help but listen to your slave master and let *him* make your choices for you. And you will live the rest of your life just as you are ... *unless* (and all God's People said, "unless") ... Someone Else is living in there *with you* Who is your "New Master" making your choices for you ... and you're listening to *Him*!

Now, I still know what you're thinking, "That's the most ridiculous thing I've ever heard of! How could something like *that* ever happen?"

You just don't know the God Who created you. Keep reading.

So, here you are ... walking around on God's green Earth in a physically alive body with a spirit as stone-cold dead as a door nail. But *you* didn't get the memo. Therefore, you think you're really *somebody.* A cool dude. The Kingpin! *But Jesus* is trying to get His Truth to you of who you *really* are. You're a lost son of the first Adam who desperately needs "The Second Adam" (Jesus) to *Save* you from yourself, your sin, and the penalty for your sins.

> *"For as the Father raiseth up the dead,*
> *and quickeneth them; even so the Son*
> *quickeneth whom He will"*
>
> (JOHN 5:21).

In this life, you must either bow to God ... or be god. And you make a very pitiful god. You may be a pretty big frog in your little pond, *but* try as you may, you will *never* be able to become the "god" of God.

When Adam and Eve sinned, they immediately felt the sting of guilt, shame, and fear. They were afraid of God and tried to run away from Him ... but they couldn't. Just like them, *you* are naked before Holy God with all of your sin exposed and condemning you. And although you may never admit it to anyone, deep inside, you're ashamed of your sin and afraid of God too.

Like Adam and Eve, *you're* running away from a confrontation with God. The wicked flee when no man pursueth. Newsflash! You can't do it either. You're running away from *The One* Who is "The Divine Solution" to all of your guilt, shame, and fear.

> *"Sin is Spiritual insanity.*
> *It is insane to rebel against Almighty God"*
>
> ---
>
> (JACK GRAHAM).

At this point in your life, you're just a lost sheep ... who needs a shepherd. Well, let me highly recommend to you my Shepherd – The Good Shepherd, Jesus.

> *"For I know that my Redeemer liveth!"*
>
> ---
>
> (JOB 19:25).

When God asked Adam, "Where art thou, Adam?", God knew where Adam was. God just wanted to make sure that *Adam* knew where he was. In a heartbeat, he was *a long way* from God. And you (Adam's great, great, great ...) took your first breath a long way from God too. And now, *you* know.

My Friend, you have a very grave problem – you're headed for the grave. You are infected with a deadly virus. It's the disease of sin, and you are terminal! If you doubt me, just look at a picture of yourself taken twenty, thirty, forty or fifty years ago. You're slowly dying under God's judgment of sin with every breath you take. So much for "havin' a nice day."

You were in the loins of Adam when he rebelled and sinned against God, and Adam has passed his spiritually dead, morally bankrupt condition down to *you.* You have gone astray from your birth and have turned to your own devious way. Your sins have put you under the sentence of death – from God.

At this point in your life, you belong to satan ... and he's headed for hell! So, how can you escape?

(Hmmm).

The second way I know you arrived into this world "spiritually dead" is because *I* was born a lost sinner just like you. For the first thirty-one years of my life, I lived in the very clutches of satan ... and didn't know it. How could this be? Jesus tells us. In John 8:44, Jesus says that satan "abode not in the truth, because there is no truth in him. When he speaketh a lie, he speaketh of his own; for he is a liar, and the father of it."

There's our answer. The devil is a liar! He lied to Eve, he lied to me, and he's still lying to all of us (including you) all the time about everything. Satan has multitudinous methods of deceit. That slimy serpent tells you the most outlandish lies, and then has the unashamed audacity to hiss, "I'm your best friend ... so you can trussssssst *me."* Right.

So, be forewarned. As you read, you will feel uneasy, undone, stressed, and distressed. You will feel as if there is a war going on in your soul. There is. Satan is screaming at you, "Don't believe that rubbish! You're too smart for fairy tales and myths. *No one* believes that stuff anymore. Nope, you're happy just the way you are."

MOLLY MCCOY

"Professing themselves to be wise, they became fools"

(ROMANS 1:22).

So, I already know what you're thinking, "This book is going to be all about *theology*, and I'm not into that stuff."

Oh, really? In the final analysis, theology is simply what you believe about God.

Now, you're saying, "Well, count me out. I never even *think* about God."

Newsflash! You are constantly thinking about and listening to "god" – *your* god. At this point, satan is the evil one controlling you and every area of your life. But you say, "Who cares, I'd rather have a blast with satan's crowd than be bored to death with you fuddy-duddy Christians."

Well, go ahead ... live it up with satan and his evil hooligans here on Planet Earth. But I must warn you, it's going to take *all* of Eternity for you to live it down ... down there.

I know where you are in life right now. I talk to people just like you all the time. The enemy of your soul has you blindly following *him*. One of ole slewfoot's favorite lies that he likes to feed people is that they are living in the "real world." I tried telling a tattooed young man about Jesus once who fiercely rejected by insisting that *he* lived in the *real world* ... not some "made-up-Jesus-world."

That young man is going to die one day, and *then,* he's going to find out just how "real" this passing temporal world really was. The devil does *not* want him to know the Truth – that he is *headed for* "The Real World" ... where Jesus Christ is LORD and on His Throne!

Satan doesn't want that young man to "see" the day that he *will* stand before the Lord Jesus (the God Who created him) in judgment for his sins. Oh no, the master liar loves to deceive people into thinking that the "fun" they're having in this "real world" is all there is. If they only knew!

That young man, enslaved by satan, is the reason my Lord "Redeemed" me and sent me out into this *unreal world* with His "Real Truth." Jesus sent me to that young man that day, and now ... He has sent me to *you*. If you think the warnings of the Surgeon General are daunting, just wait 'til you hear *God's*!

Truth is, this "real world" is just a test. The Lord Jesus is testing you to see if you will choose to continue going satan's way, *or* if you will choose to go *His* Way instead. The choice is yours alone. You either live for God, or you live for the devil. You can either have a good time with your friends in this world now, *or* you can have the Joy of Jesus in His World now *and forever*! You can either let Jesus use you to build His Eternal Kingdom, *or* you can continue letting satan use you up!

You must decide to choose to please God (the One Who Loves you more than anyone else) *or* choose to please satan (the evil one who hates you more than anyone else). When you choose to please God, He rewards you with Eternal Blessings! *But* when you choose to please satan, *he* plagues you with demonic curses as he wastes your God-given life on fleeting, worthless pursuits.

> *"Now yells louder ... but later lasts longer!"*
> ───────────
> (LEVI LUSKO).

So ... would you rather live in satan's world or in Jesus' World? Nooooo contest. You are convinced that you would rather live in satan's world. Why? Because you just haven't taken the long look ... yet. And only the Lord Jesus can give you the "Spiritual Eyes" you need to see into **Eternity.**

"When you're young, you're a 'short-term thinker.' Every-thing is all about NOW!"

(TONY EVANS).

Satan has you so short-sighted that you can't see beyond the ground beneath your feet. You are choosing to live your life "your way" – seizing the day and grabbing the pleasure of the moment. *And* you're lovin' it ... right now. *But God* is of-fering you a Divine telephoto lens so that you can look beyond the words on the pages of this book and catch a glimpse of ... *FOREVER!*

When you accept God's offer, He will reveal to you His Glo-rious Son – the One you can't see at the moment. His Name is Jesus, and only *He* can give you the Supernatural Vision you need to "see" into the realities of the *Spiritual World* – where you are presently being held prisoner in the demonic realm. *Mercy Me!*

"For the Son of Man is come to "Save"
that which was lost (to satan)"

(MATTHEW 18:11).

The devil has a wonderful plan for your life (at least, *he* thinks so). Satan wants to keep you going on down the road you're going down so that you will end up wrecking your life or going to prison ... and eventually going to the permanent prison – hell. He knows there's no "going over the wall at mid-night" in *that one*!

Truth is, satan hates you and has a devilishly horrible plan for your life. He is the ultimate shifty used-car salesman. Sa-tan sells you a shined-up "junk life" that deteriorates at a very rapid rate as you drive it down the road of life. Give the devil a ride, and he will hi-jack the car and drive you places you *don't* want to go. If you doubt me, just wait. With satan at the helm of your life, *your* ship is headed into *the perfect storm*. It's just a matter of time.

> *"False gods always abuse their worshipers*
> *and harm their followers"*
>
> ---
> (DAVID JEREMIAH).

The one thing my Daddy said to me more than anything else was one word: "Think!" Now I'm passing his wise counsel on to *you*. "THINK!" *Think* about what you're doing and where it will take you – to a good job or to jail ... to Heaven or to hell! There are many things in your life that are very important, *but* nothing – and I mean *nothing* – is more important than where you are going to spend Eternity ... because you *are* going "somewhere."

Decisions determine Destiny! We make our choices, and then our choices make *us – forever*! Every choice I have ever chosen; every decision I have ever made in my life, I will live with forever. Our choices and decisions shape our *Eternal* future. There is *"something* going on" on this Earth today (and in your life today) that will last *forever.* And satan's greatest victory is blinding us to that truth – *God's* Truth.

There's not a moment of time that isn't of great importance ... to God – "The Watcher." The Great I AM says, "I AM watching you!" God didn't send you to Planet Earth for no reason.

However, you insist on letting wicked satan just waste your life ... which is of infinite value to the God Who created you in His Image for *Himself.* You are sacrificing that which will last for *all Eternity* on the altar of that which you want *right now.* And because you aren't thankful for what you have today, you will never be happy with anything you ever get in the future. But the Lord is watching you. *He* is the One Who caused you to pick up this book and start reading. God always has a purpose.

He always has a reason – an Eternal Reason.

*"What you do in life
echoes into Eternity!"*

(LAMPLIGHTER THEATER).

After all these years, I have decided that three of the surest things in life are taxes, brake jobs, and death … and in that order. I have also concluded that it's the first two that help bring about the third. So be forewarned, my Friend, that whatever the cause, you have a date with **death** in your future. And when you die and stand before the God of this Universe, you will finally *know* Who He is. And you will also know who you are.

I wrote this book to bring you into the Lord's Holy Presence *now* … while He is still reaching out His nail-pierced Hand to you as your Saviour. If you refuse Him *now*, you will one day have to stand before Him in judgment for your sins. And all the hosts of Heaven and hell are watching you to see what you are going to do. *Mercy Me!*

*"For God speaketh once, yea twice,
yet man perceiveth it not"*

(JOB 33:14).

My prayer is that the Lord will reveal the Majesty of His Glory to you in a *Supernatural* way as you stand before Him right now … and you *are* standing before Him right now. You can't see Him, but I can guarantee you: *He* sees *you. And* He sees right through you!

"Am I a God at hand, saith the Lord,

and not a God afar off?
Can any hide himself
in secret places
that I shall not see him?"

(JEREMIAH 23:23-24).

The One you need more than anyone else is Someone you can't even see. It's *Jesus* Who has more Love and Power than anyone else to meet your need and change you. But *you* know that you have "issues" in your life that other people don't know about. I have news for you: You have deep issues in your life *(and in your soul)* that even *you* don't know about. Only Jesus can (and will!) deal with them *all*. You receive the *Spiritually* healing, *Saving* Power of the Lord in His Presence. You are in His Presence. So, why aren't you "Saved"?

Answer: Because no one has ever told you before that you are living in God's Presence every moment of your life! Nor have they told you that you *need* to be "Saved" – or *how* to be "Saved." *You* think that all you need is just a new start ... when what you *really* need is a new heart. So take heart, Dear Heart, and keep reading.

You, my Friend, are a "diamond in the rough." You just need the right "Touch" to bring out your hidden luster. Well, the Master Diamond Cutter is here to make you fit into His Eternal Kingdom ... by making you fit *for* His Eternal Kingdom. His Name is Jesus Christ, and His cutting-edge knife is ready. It's called: The Sword of The Spirit – the Word of God – wielded by The Living Word (Jesus).

"Jesus answered and said unto them:
Ye do ere, not knowing the Scriptures,
nor the Power of God!"

(MATTHEW 22:29).

Some people say, "God said it, I believe it, and that settles it." But they are wrong. The truth is: When God says it ... *THAT* settles it – whether *you* believe it, or not. Just because you choose to call the Bible "a fairy-tale book" doesn't bother God. He sits on His Throne in Heaven and laughs at you ... because His Word is settled in Heaven *forever*! *You* will pass away, but God's Word is as Eternal as He is.

The reason you and your fellow-worldlings think that this world is the "real world" is because it's the only world you have. We Christians are a mystery to you because we live in two Worlds at the same time. Yep, we are citizens of America, but more important than being a citizen of any Country on Earth, we are Citizens of God's Eternal Heavenly Kingdom. Now, *that's* the Real World! And Jesus will never get tired of me and send me back to satan's world. "Thank You, Lord!"

We Christians are just here singing the Lord's Song in a foreign land (and America gets more foreign everyday). This world is not our home, we're jest apassin' through. But while we're here, our God-given mission is to "be Jesus" to this world He came to *Redeem*.

Back in the '60's in America, the hippies were counter-culture. Today, it's us Christians. And the rest of the world just can't figure us out. They are constantly glancing over their shoulder at us and asking, "Who *are* those guys?"

We are a mystery to them because we live in a different World. "*But God,* Who is rich in Mercy ... hath quickened us together with Christ ... and made us sit together in Heavenly Places in Christ Jesus" (Ephesians 2:4-6). From there, we live here in Jesus' Up-Side-Down-World: Jesus gives us Eternal Life through His death. Jesus frees us to be His slave. Jesus gives us His Joy in hard times. We go down to go up. We love the unlovely. We Praise through tears. We lose to win. We give to get. We die to live. We are strong when we are weak. We are great when we serve. We give Blessings for curses. We humble ourselves to be exalted.

We "hear" an unseen Person speaking to us Whom we profess to be The King of an unseen Kingdom! And get this, we even speak to *Him* and actually believe that He hears us. *And* answers us! How much weirder can you get? But to a Born-Again Christian, the Supernatural is natural. We sacrifice our lives for our Lord Jesus, and spend our time, energy, and money on *His* Eternal Cause.

So, why do we do all these *strange* things? Ah, we know a Truth that you worldlings don't know (yet). In the unseen "Spiritual World" there are *only* two kingdoms – God's Righteous Eternal Kingdom and satan's evil kingdom of death. Those are your *only* two options. There is *no middle ground. None!* Every soul born into this world arrives in satan's kingdom of spiritual death. *No exceptions. None!* Satan has power over you, and that power is sin. You were born in sin and in satan's power.

The liberals of today want as many people as possible claiming to be "a victim." Well, they can relax. We are *all* victims … of satan! Some people say that satan's followers are "brain-dead," but they are wrong. Truth is, those confused folks aren't really brain-dead … they're just "spirit-dead." Without the Spirit of Christ 'Living' in *your* spirit, you're just a walking dead man. *Mercy Me!*

Jesus proclaims, "He who is not with Me is against Me!" (Matthew 12:30). But you think that *you* are the exception.

You say, "I'm not with Jesus, but I don't belong to satan either … so I'm OK." *(Hmmm).*

Well, the truth is that you, my Friend, are a "spirit-man" who is *merely living* in a "flesh-man." So, who is the god of your spirit-man?

You say, "No one. I'm my own god."

That's interesting. That means that when your flesh-man dies, it's up to your spirit-man to take care of *himself* for all Eternity. That should be even more interesting.

You need a friend who will lovingly tell you that there's only one God per universe – and *you're* not Him! *But* your worst enemy keeps telling you that evolution is true so that you won't believe in the unseen "Spiritual Realm." Therefore, you believe that you're just a physical body which evolved from animals, and when you're dead, you're ... just dead. You have no Eternal spirit, no meaning, and no purpose in life.

I feel so sorry for you, because *that* is the number-one lie satan *wants* you to believe. And since you are in total agreement with the one you belong to, anything he tells you to believe or do ... you dutifully do. Trust me, ole slewfoot does a victory dance every time he gets someone (like you) to believe that their life ends in the grave.

However, since you don't believe in the Spiritual Realm, then you are only allowed to have a body that is physically alive *but* unable to think, speak, make decisions, or love anyone ... because that would require a soul (mind, will, emotions). Your "mind" is in your invisible soul. It merely *uses* your brain to think. Your brain is the hard-drive – your mind is the software. Dreams are thoughts your mind thinks while your brain is asleep. Your physical brain needs sleep, but your mind resides in the Spiritual Realm where sleep isn't needful (ask any insomniac).

Your conscience is also in your invisible soul. Without it,

you don't know right from wrong. Prayer is invisible, as well, and takes place in your soul with the unseen God Who created you (once you have received *Christ's* Spirit into your dead spirit – making you "Spiritually Alive!"). *But*, if you don't have a soul, you are unable to have "a Relationship" with God. So, when you believe in evolution, your only option is to be an atheist. And, as an atheist, you have no God, no spirit, no soul, no Eternal Life, no Godly wisdom, and no ability to make moral decisions.

Now, I know what you're thinking, "You're wrong about me. I *do* make moral decisions."

Well, good. Then, you have just admitted that you *do* have a soul – which is in your spirit-man who exists in the Spiritual Realm ... where God is. Congratulations, you have just taken your first step to the right side of reality. Take another step, my Friend, and you will "see" that you don't merely *have* a soul ... you *are* a soul. Thoughts, speech, decisions, moral choices, and love are all invisible. They come from your invisible soul which exists in the invisible *Spiritual Realm*. Welcome to "Jesus' World."

(**NOTE:** Over my lifetime, I have watched several people die, and I have noticed that death isn't just a matter of some of your bodily functions ceasing to function. Nope, death occurs when *all* of your bodily functions immediately and simultaneously stop *at the very moment* your spirit (soul) leaves your body! You have just departed this world and entered into the "Spiritual World" ... and left your Earthsuit behind.)

Let me ask you another question, "Who is 'the one' who is spiritually against Jesus?"

Right. In the Spiritual Realm, satan's kingdom of wickedness is always waging war against Jesus' Kingdom of Righteousness. "The mystery of iniquity" is no mystery to us Christians. We know that the devil is the evil one behind all the sin of this world. *People* aren't really warring against each other – two "Spiritual Kingdoms" are warring against each other! Satan snookered Adam out of Planet Earth ... and it jolly well looks like it. The seed of the woman and the seed of the serpent are still going at it today (Genesis 3:15). *Mercy Me!*

(**NOTE:** As you look at the things people do in this world, ask yourself, "Is this from the True God of Love and Life, *or* is this from the cruel demon-god of hate and death?" Start looking through (and behind) the things you see, and you will discover which God (god) is their source. You will no longer have to wonder why a person will take weapons and kill scores of innocent people. He is just obeying the orders of his "master." Satan's greatest achievement is to get the Crown of God's Creation (man) to take the life of another Crown of God's Creation. You will also know why a Christian will risk his own life in order to tell lost people about Jesus. He is also obeying the orders of *his* "Master." God's greatest achievement was sending His own Son to die on a Cross to give Eternal Life to those who *believe* and *receive*.)

Now, since you have *not* been granted your own little "kingdom of you," then you *must* be in one of these two Spiritual Kingdoms. You're not with Jesus ... so you're with satan. You're in satan's kingdom, and he has sealed you there with sin. *But* ... we Christians have been *miraculously* liberated from the devil's evil kingdom of death. Wouldn't *you* like to be *miraculously* liberated too? Just asking.

OLE SLEWFOOT

"And Paul said, I would to God that not only thou,
but also all that hear me this day,
were both almost and altogether such as I,
except for these bonds"

(ACTS 26:29).

As you've been barreling through life at break-neck speed, have you ever had a head-on collision with the Lord Jesus Christ? He is LORD of all lords and KING above all kings, politicians, and lawmakers. He is the Ultimate Promise-Keeper.

Satan, on the other hand, is the best April Fool's Day trickster in the history of the world. Just about the time he gets you believing his lie that everything that glitters really *is* gold, he screams, "April Fool!" ... and it all turns to mud in your hand.

If you have never believed the Truth of the Gospel of Jesus Christ, you are not only an April Fool, you're ... well ... satan's "fooled-one." "The fool hath said in his heart: There is no God" (Psalm 53:1). There's a better way than going through life as "satan's fooled-one." Hint: It's living a great life as Jesus' wise Disciple.

Now, I hate to have to tell you this, but I must. Satan doesn't want you to know it, but he has also fooled you into being his slave. Yep, and you're falling right in line with his scheme. He's got you right where he wants you. You have willfully chosen to live your life as far from God's Love as you can possibly get ... so that you can live your life as "free" from God's Law as you can possibly get. Right? Of course.

It's not that you *can't* believe in God (deep in your heart you *know* He exists, otherwise *you* wouldn't exist), it's that you don't *want to* believe in God ... because then *He* would be Boss, and you want to be your own boss. Right? Of course.

Ole slewfoot's lie to Eve was that she would be better off free from God, and apparently, satan doesn't need to come up with any new material. Nope, you're co-operating perfectly. So, you got rid of God in order to get rid of God's moral standard. Satan loves it! *Now* you're "free" to live your life by *his immoral* standard: Katie, bar the door! Or translated: Anything goes!

However, even as you refuse to bow your knee to the Lord Jesus, you are bowing your whole life to your master, satan, who keeps telling you what a *free spirit* you are ... when all along he has you bound up in his chains of sin. You aren't really free, you're just 'on parole' from the devil. Yep, and sadly, you learned a lot of his devious ways while 'doing time' in satan's Alcatraz. But don't despair, I used to be a prisoner there myself. *Mercy Me!*

In 1865, Abraham Lincoln abolished slavery in America, right? Wrong. Slavery is still thriving here because millions of Americans are *still* in bondage ... to satan. Every person on the face of this Earth belongs to either the Lord Jesus or satan. And now, my Friend, you know who *you* belong to.

"Verily, verily, I say unto you, Whosoever committeth sin is the servant (slave) of sin."
Signed: Jesus

(JOHN 8:34).

Now, I know what you're thinking, "Hey Dude, I may not be perfect, but I'm certainly *not* satan's slave."

Oh, yeah? Well, the next time he tells you to do something

that you *know* is totally *against God's* Commands, *but* you really want to do it … see what happens. I rest my case.

> *"Stop fighting the devil … and yield to Jesus.*
> *Why fight a battle already lost when you can enjoy a*
> *'Victory' already won!"*

(ADRIAN ROGERS).

Satan's objective is to totally eradicate "the Knowledge of God" from your heart and mind. Then, with no God, you're left with just yourself – whom that ole devil is well able to control. You can either be a son of God or a slave of satan … you choose.

> *"The world says, 'Happy are the free!' Jesus says,*
> *'Happy are the Holy.'"*

(DAVID JEREMIAH)

Another reason worldlings think we Christians are weird is because not only do we live in two worlds at the same time, but two *People* live in our body at the same time. *Really!* See what I mean? They call us crazy, but that doesn't bother us. We just smile and say, "You're right. I *am* crazy. I'm crazy about my Lord Jesus! And Jesus (Who "lives!" in me) tells me to have compassion on my neighbor by meeting his need. You are my neighbor, and *you need JESUS*!"

You, my Friend, are the guy who has been beaten-up by satan and is now dying by the side of the road … *until Jesus* comes along … sees you lying there and knows that you have been mortally wounded by the sting of sin. He knows that you need a Miracle to save you. You need "The Miracle Worker." *This* is *your* day! *Jesus* is The Miracle Worker! Jesus is passing by, and when Jesus passes by ... *everything* changes. In one way of another, you will *never* be the same again.

> *"I knelt down a tramp ... and stood up a LADY!*
> *I knelt down a prostitute ... and stood up Jesus' Virgin!"*

(IRIS BLUE).

Jesus Christ was the most controversial Person to ever walk this Earth ... and He meant to be. Jesus came to bring radical change to our world. And at *this* moment, He is looking straight at *you* ... and *me*! He's watching to see if I will be your friend, have compassion on you and meet your need. What you need is for *someone* to carry you to the foot of Jesus' Eternal Cross where "The Great **I AM**" is waiting to compassionately meet your deepest *Spiritual* need.

This is my chance to "be Jesus" to you, my Friend, because this book is "Jesus" breaking satan's chains of bondage he has had on you all your life. *The Lord Jesus* is the One setting you free from the liar who has kept you shackled in sin and death from the day you were born. *Mercy Me!*

> *"These are written that ye might believe that Jesus is*
> *The Christ, the Son of God; and that believing*
> *ye might have 'Life' through His Name!"*

(JOHN 20:31).

Another way the devil lies to us is by telling us we're all OK. You're OK, I'm OK, everybody's OK ... so don't worry about it.

Most husbands know that when his wife simply answers "nothing" when he asks her what's wrong ... he is in deep trouble. Satan, your evil mistress, keeps telling you that "nothing is wrong." So you better believe ... *you* is in deep trouble!

That demonic trouble-maker is the enemy of your soul, and he twists your mind with his "slave psychology." Ole slewfoot tells you that you should never have any negative, depressing thoughts. That's bad for you. Never call those wicked things you're doing "sins." Nope, there's really no such thing as "sin" anymore. Therefore, nothing to feel guilty about.

No siree, those liberals done took a survey, and people the world over voted whole-heartedly *against* sin! Yep, sin has been voted *out*. Yea! No more being *a sinner.* A little moral-ly-challenged maybe ... but that's no big deal. So, don't think twice, it's alright.

People everywhere have not only voted out sin, but they have also voted out *God* (the One Who calls sin "sin") over and over again ... naturally. The idea that there really *is* a Supreme Almighty God Who created everything and will one day judge everyone is *so* ridiculous that it's almost laughable. Truly in-telligent people know that God doesn't really exist. Nope, ev-erything and everyone just "somehow" evolved out of ... well ... something. And *that's* scientific fact.

Chuck Missler says, "Their Big Bang theory is this: First there was nothing, and then ... it exploded into everything!" (Right – *and all by itself!*)

> (**NOTE:** Morality and marriage have been redefined by puny man ... who was *created* by the very God he's redefining. Go figure.)

With satan's permission you are now finally free to go ahead and seer your conscience. You don't need "guilt" any-more. No way, just do *whatever* and don't worry about it.

Feel *good* about yourself! Everybody knows that you just make your soul "sick" by denying it the passions it desires. *So* ... the secret to a "happy soul" is to give it *anything* and *everything* it desires. Yes!

Just keep on being a "free spirit" living "in the world" ... so that you can leave God out of everything in your life. Then, spend your time thinking about how liberated, free, and happy you are. And for sure don't ever think about your death and what's going to happen to you *then*. No, don't ever scare yourself by thinking about *that*. Watch horror movies and watch other people die, but don't ever think about the fact that one day (sooner or later) it will be *your* turn to die.

Don't waste a single minute of your precious time thinking about running into this God you are presently rejecting ... and what He might do to *you*! There's not a chance in *this world* or *the next* that God's Justice will *ever* have to be satisfied. Nope, you're getting away with *everything*.

> *"I said therefore unto you,*
> *that ye shall die in your sins:*
> *for if ye believe not that* **I AM** *He,*
> *ye shall die in your sins."*
> *Signed: Jesus*
> ───────
> (JOHN 8:24).

You have chosen your path ... which means you have also chosen your Destiny. And that ole deceiver doesn't want you ever choosing to think about the fact that there is a death to die, a God to meet, and a Judgment to face – a Judgment as sure as death. With every heartbeat, you get closer to your last one.

> *"Eventually, all the toys go back in the box,*
> *and the game is over"*

(ALISTAIR BEGG).

"Then shall the dust (your body) return to the earth as it was,
and the spirit shall return unto God Who gave it"

(ECCLESIASTES 12:7).

So, have you ever thought about it? What do you think is going to happen to *you* when you take *your* last breath and leave Planet Earth for good?

Aren't you glad you kept reading? I know what you're thinking, "This is the most depressing book I've ever read. Why would anyone write a book about such morbid stuff?"

Hey, do you want to dare to "be Jesus", or not? Jesus was crucified on a Cross. And that's exactly what's going to have to happen to *you* ... if you want to "be Jesus" on this Earth. Fallen man is so corrupt and so evil that he can't possibly be reformed. Death is the only cure!

Are you still glad you decided to continue reading? How confused are you right now? Very?

Well, I'll tell you up-front, I'm not like many preachers today who absolutely refuse to "offend" *anyone* with the Truth of the Gospel of Jesus Christ. I will not remain silent while satan's slaves brazenly parade their sin and greatly offend *God,* because that greatly offends *me.* So, I don't apologize for offending that God-hating "demon-god of this world." No matter how many people love and follow him, I will resolutely stand with *my* LORD – Whom *I* love.

The Lord Jesus always tells you the Truth:

MOLLY MCCOY

"I AM The Way, The Truth and The Life!"

(JOHN 14:6).

He is the One Who is speaking to you through this book, and right now, He's asking you some very thought-provoking questions:

"Do you ever wonder if there really *is* a God? And what about Me, His Son? Who am I, *really*? Who do *you* say that I AM? Ever wondered if I really *did die* on that Cross ... and why? Do you ever consider Eternity? Ever hope there really *is* a Heaven to go to when you die? Do you ever wonder if your life has any meaning or purpose? Ever think about sin and judgment? Do you ever think about death? Hell?"

Well, not if satan has *his* way, you won't. That evil prince of the demonic world hates God; he hates the Lord Jesus; he detests the Bible; he hates Christians; he hates me, and he hates *you*! The last thing in the world the devil wants you to do is read this book. Really! He specializes in hate and lies – not Love and Truth. The only thing satan loves is keeping you blinded by his demonic darkness. So, it's entirely possible for you to read every word of this book and never "See Jesus!" – because satan absolutely *hates* giving up his slaves. *Mercy Me!*

That ole devil doesn't want you to know that you showed up on Earth in his clutches. Nope, he's so afraid you're going to wise-up and figure out that the reason you're such a sinner is because you belong to the source of all sin – *him*! He's blinding you to the Truth that the God (god) you follow on this Earth is the God (god) you will follow into *Eternity*!

Satan doesn't want you knowing that you were born in sin – lost for all Eternity and headed for the same place *he's* going. Nor does he want you to "see" your wretched condition – condemned by your sin to a Christ-less Eternity when you die ... and die you will!

God's Eternal Truth is that the chains of sin are dragging you down to hell with satan and his demons, and over the dark entrance to hell is a smoldering sign which reads:

ABANDON ALL HOPE YE WHO ENTER HERE ....
YYYYYYAAAAAAAAAAAA!

!!!!!!

"The heart of the sons of men is full of evil,
and madness is in their heart while they live,
and after that they go to the dead"

(ECCLESIASTES 9:3).

Where will *your* soul go when you die? The souls in torment are totally helpless and miserably hopeless! And in those rare moments when you think about *your* true spiritual condition, you know that in the depths of your soul, *you* are totally helpless and miserably hopeless too. You have rejected the True God. *So* ... who do you have left? You're left with your slave master, satan, who has your mind all wrapped up in chains. But your heart still knows the Truth, because God hath set ETERNITY in your heart! And your heart is giving you a flicker of hope.

If you want help, you may have it ... *now*! If you want hope, you may have it ... *now*! You will find *all* that you need in Jesus' Spiritual World at the foot of His Eternal Cross. You only get it on your spiritual knees through the *Prayer of Faith*. God will set you free! *But only* when you finally realize and admit that you *need* to be set free, *and* that you need *God* to set you free.

Satan has you in Spiritual Checkmate! *But God* is offering you a "spiritual move" that ole slewfoot is hoping you won't take. Why not give the devil the surprise of his miserable existence by listening, heeding and reverently receiving the *Truth* being sent to you from God Himself.

God has "a Call" on your life. *Now* is the time for you to respond to God's Call. God has "a Plan" for your life. His Plan right now is for you to run right-smack-dab into *Him*! *This very moment* has been designed and purposed by the Lord in order to accomplish His Will in you on this Earth. Jesus Christ is drawing you to Himself! His "Call" to you is, "Come! Follow *Me*! **I AM** the One you need."

> *"Come unto Me,*
> *all ye that labor and are heavy laden,*
> *and* **I Will** *give you rest."*
> *Signed: Jesus*
>
> (MATTHEW 11:28).

You are a stranger to this world, and you don't know why you're here or where you're going. You don't know where you're going when you die because you don't know where you came from in the first place. That's because you went to liberal schools that taught you to believe in their "religion" called *evolution*. They helped you toss God completely out of your life. Now, here you are with absolutely *nothing* to hold onto in life. Is there any wonder you just keep bouncing around all over the place?

Every lust you chase after in life will disappoint you ... except one – the lust to find your God and His Love for you. I know you, and deep in your heart you would *love* to have "Something" to hold onto in life that will *never* let you down and *never* let you go.

Truth is, you are here as a part of God's big unfolding drama on Planet Earth. But you laugh. *You* think that life is all about *you*. Life is really all about *GOD*! Yep, and deeper still, life is all about *God and you*. Once you put your new "Spiritual Glasses" on, you will be able to see that life is really all about God's Divine, Eternal Purpose He has for *you* – both now and *forever*! Today is the day that you humbled yourself and *let Him* open your spiritually blind eyes. God will not strive with your spirit forever. *But God is* "calling" you *today* ... to Himself and to His Son. Today is the day of Salvation – *your* Salvation!

Some people's motto is: Never do today what you can put off until tomorrow. Trouble is, if you keep putting certain things off long enough, the day is coming when you are going to run out of tomorrows and run into "that one long tomorrow" waiting for us all. *Then*, you will wish with all your heart and soul that you had *just one more tomorrow* left in which to give your attention to The One Whom you are standing before *now*! But it will be too bad, so sad, your Dad.

"That Tomorrow" is coming just as surely as the moments you're spending reading these words right now. It's just a matter of time. And I can guarantee you: On Judgment Day you will wish that you had been a **FANATIC** for Jesus Christ!!

"Behold, I come quickly; and My reward is with Me,
to give every man according as his work shall be!"
Signed: Jesus

(REVELATION 22:12).

"You can't just tip your hat to the Lord Jesus.
You must bow your knee to Him!"

(ADRIAN ROGERS).

"At the Name of Jesus every knee shall bow ...
and every tongue shall confess that Jesus Christ is LORD
to the Glory of God the Father!"

(PHILIPPIANS 2:10-11).

You may be having your Saturday-night-fling *right now,* *but* Son Day morning *is* coming, and you will open your satan-drugged eyes to see The Son of God upon His Throne of Judgment! What you do with Jesus *now* will determine what He does with you *then.* There are really only two days on your calendar – this day and "THAT DAY!"

"Now ... or then. Here ... or there. You *will* bow to Jesus Christ – either as your King or as your Judge!" Signed: God.

I have set before you this day life and death. You can choose to love God and live *forever, or* you can choose to love this world and it's "demon-god" and die an **eternal death.** You choose.

"One way to make sure crime doesn't pay would be to let the government run it" (Ronald Reagan).

Well, unfortunately, satan is the evil one running the "crime syndicate" all over the world, and he makes sure it pays his slaves very well ... at least, *they* think so. But how much good will all their wealth do them when they die and face God in Judgment?

If you really dig the things of the devil, I have news for you ... the devil is gleefully digging your grave – your *eternal* grave! Like Judas, satan gives you the kiss of death. And some day *God* will give you His "Final Call." Could this be it? You're a drowning man ... and you know it. *But God* is reaching out His Divine Hand of Love, Mercy, and Grace to you. *And* He is offering you a Gift – the Hand of Faith. It's free. So, take it and use it to grab the Hand of the Saviour, Jesus, Who Loves you with an *Everlasting Love.*

You may be going under for the last time, *but Jesus* is giving you one last chance to give it all over to Him ... and let Him *Save* you. You are no match for satan, and you will never be able to free yourself from his stranglehold-grip. Your days on this Earth are numbered. So, you had better start applying your heart to wisdom – *today.* It's time you quit making such a hash out of your life and let Jesus make a "Miracle Transformation" out of it ... before it's too late. *Eternally* too late!

Ole slewfoot prowls about seeking *someone* to devour. But, in order to devour this *someone* (I'm not calling any names here), he must first lure them into his web of sin. So, satan offers this *someone* the perfect "bait" they just can't resist. This *someone* bites the bait, and – Zap! – they're stuck in satan's web of sin and can't free themselves ... no matter how hard they try. Yep ... *someone.*

"Welcome to my parlor" said the spider to the fly – just before he trapped him, killed him and devoured the poor unsuspecting fly. And that's exactly what satan does to you ... because you, Dear Heart, are the "unsuspecting fly" in the vortex of his evil web. *You* see a world of endless delights. The demonic spiderman sees lunch! Are you on satan's menu today? Of course, you are. Do you love his sticky delights that keep you trapped in his deadly web – his house of horrors? Of course, you do.

"First sin fascinates, then it assassinates. First sin thrills, and then it kills. Every kick has a kick-back" (Adrian Rogers). *But Jesus* is the best "Spider Swatter" there is. Don't keep endlessly cleaning out spider webs. No, let Jesus kill the spider! Aren't you tired of letting satan eat *you* for lunch? Just asking.

Ole slewfoot has plenty of schemes to keep his slaves stuck in his sticky web of bondage. Many people today have a gambling addiction. Maybe you're one. You know it's destroying your life, but you just can't fling that monkey off your back.

"You can kick your sin out of the front door, and it will just run around the house and climb in a basement window!"

(ADRIAN ROGERS).

Satan's dice are loaded with sin and sorrow, and his de-mon-marked deck is stacked against you. If you're following satan, you are gambling your *entire Eternity* on a loser that is headed for hell – *forever!* The odds are much better for ending up in Heaven following Jesus. In fact, you can bet your Eternal Soul on it!

It is often said that God will be a debtor to no man. When you serve God, He always repays you. Since satan is "the evil imitator of God," he does the same thing. Serve satan and see what you get. The wages of satan is death. Little by little, he will steal, kill and destroy *everything* in your life.

"WELCOME TO SATAN'S WORLD!"

The devil isn't living rent-free in your soul, you know. Not hard-ly. He is extracting an extremely high price from you – your re-lationships, your health, your possessions, your joy, your sanity, your very soul, and most importantly – your Eternal Life!

The world you're living in is doomed and self-destructing, but ole slewfoot doesn't want you to know it. Nope, he's not about to tell you that you're doing 90 miles-an-hour down a dead-end street – heading for death, the grave, judgment, and Eternal damnation! You get around faster driving your flashy sports car, but you *still* don't know where you're going. And the devil wants to keep you that way – strapped into a dead-end life with *him* hitting the accelerator. *Mercy Me!*

"Satan sails a sinking ship; he rules a doomed domain"

(ADRIAN ROGERS).

Satan doesn't want you ever thinking those deep spiritual thoughts about yourself, your life, and your *ultimate* Destiny. Nor does he want you waking up and smelling the smoke before it's too late – *Eternally* too late! Oh no, he wants to keep you thinking only about this present physical world that is passing away with each heartbeat.

The enemy of your soul is devilishly happy when all you're thinking about is having a "good time" and the party this Saturday night: "Who's going to be there? What will we drink? What will we smoke? What 'all' will we do? What will I dare to wear? Who will I impress? Will the cops show up?"

When these are the kinds of thoughts that flood your mind, satan has done his job – and done it well. He passed the test, and *you* flunked. I guess that makes you satan's flunky ... and he loves it. But Someone Else is watching you floundering around in satan's world ... and *He* Loves *you*.

Aren't you ready to wise-up and ace God's Test? Don't you ever slow down long enough to ask yourself those hard staring-you-in-the-face questions like:

> Is *this* all there is to life?
>
> Is *this place* all there is?
>
> Is *this time* all I've got?
>
> Are *these friends* all I'll ever have?
>
> Is anyone's love *real*?
>
> My Grandpa is so old and decrepit ... is life really just a cruel joke after all?
>
> Is death the end ... of *everything*?

Satan is desperately trying to keep you from wising up and learning the Truth: Your earthly life is just preparation for your future – your *Eternal Future*! The enemy of your soul doesn't want you wisely considering the fact that your heart isn't going to keep beating forever, and when it takes its last beat, you're headed for an encounter with your Creator, aka the Lord Jesus Christ!

Ole slewfoot doesn't want you prepared to meet your Maker. Nope, satan wants to keep you consumed with foolishly chasing after every thrill and every pleasure you can possibly squeeze out of this life on Planet Earth. The demonic party-beast tells you that you're *really livin'*! *But Jesus* knows the Truth: You're *really dead* – spiritually dead. And when you're taking your last breath, you will finally realize that *none of it* had *any* **Eternal value!**

> (**NOTE:** Born-Again Christians *know* beyond any doubt that when we breathe our last breath here, the only thing that matters *then* is how many people will be in Heaven because we told them about *Jesus. Yes!*)

You live in your flesh and think that your physical body is where your life is ... because it is *so "ALIVE!"* – right now. But truth be told, *that* is where *death* is – just you wait. You can't elude death with all the yogurt, vitamins, and wrinkle cream in your health food store. In the end, your flesh is not your friend. It's really your worst enemy ... apart from the Power of Christ to control it.

Your true *life* is in your "spirit-man" who lives *within* your flesh ... but only *if* you have received "*God's* Life" through the death of His Son, Jesus, on the Cross. If you die without *God's Life* in you ... you have no life left. *Mercy Me!*

Nope, ole slewfoot has managed to keep you in his evil kingdom of darkness and death your entire physical life. And *now,* it's over ... *forever!* Oh, you will still exist, but in a place of eternal death (Mark 9:42-48). There really *is* a Heaven to gain and a hell to shun. God wants you in Heaven with Him. The devil wants you in hell with him. So, whatcha gonna do, bad boy, when they come for *you*?

"No servant can serve two masters."
Signed: Jesus

(LUKE 16:13).

"A lost man is born into the natural world, he is blind to the 'Spiritual World,' and he is bound to the material world. Therefore, he cannot receive the things of God"

(ADRIAN ROGERS).

(Hmmm).

Now, I know what you're thinking, "Then ... there's no hope for me."

Not so fast. Let's hear what the Lord Jesus has to say,

"No man can come unto Me, except the Father Who hath sent Me draw him"

(JOHN 6:44).

Ah, there *is* hope! And Hope has a Name. So, if you're feeling a warm tug on your heart as you read, that's *God the Father* ... graciously giving you the chance to exercise your power of choice ... to choose *Him*!

However, you may be the guy always looking for a *person* who can fix all the problems in your life ... if such a person exists. But you have decided he doesn't, or else he's coming from the stars, Mars, or the moon ... because he sure hasn't shown up in *your* life yet.

Well, what if I told you that Mr. Fix-it has indeed arrived, and He's ringing your doorbell right now. Really! But instead of fixing all the problems in your life, He's going to fix *you* ... because *you* are your problem. You can't see well because you're short-sighted, you're hard of hearing because "someone" has his dirty fingers in your ears, you've got heart trouble, you suffer from demon-depression, and you're spiritually dead ... just to mention a few. In short, you're the broken-down property of satan.

So, are you ready to open your broken-heart's door to Mr. Fix-it? When you do, you will see the Lord Jesus standing there ... smiling at you! And trust me, there isn't anything in the entire Universe (or your broken-down life) that the Lord Jesus can't fix. Hallelujah!

However, I must warn you that if you try opening the door of your heart to Jesus ... beware. Your evil landlord, who is presently holding you captive in his castle of horrors, will yell, "SHUT THAT DOOR!! Didn't I tell you not to let any Strangers in here! To the dungeon on bread and water for *you*! (Oh yeah ... what I'm gonna do to that stupid slave.)"

Now, it's up to you. Who are you going to listen to?

Well, ask yourself how truly joyful and content you are living under your present slave master. If you are going through life without the Lord Jesus, you're going through life with a broken heart. So, just admit it: You're a sad person looking for someone to love you.

You're looking for JESUS! He heals the broken-hearted. Jesus reaches His hand of Love through your porcupine quills and touches your broken heart with His Love. *He comes to you!* Jesus brings with Him His Supernatural Life, His Divine Love, and healing in His Wings. When the Lord Jesus touches your soul with His *Irresistible Love*, your heart will melt like a snowball in the August sun. You'll see.

However, that won't happen *until* you open your heart and let Jesus in. Until you *let* Jesus "Save" you, you will be broken and miserable. God created you for Himself. So, wise up. Listen to the Voice of God's Holy Spirit Who is whispering to your broken heart, "Mr. Fix-it, aka the Lord Jesus, is the One Who created you. So, He certainly knows how to fix you – completely, spiritually, *Eternally*!"

Up until now, you've been listening to the wrong voice. You're listening to "the deceiver." He is *not* your friend, *but* he has managed to convince you that he is actually on your side … yesssssssss! What a joke. Truth is, that slimy enemy of your soul is desperately trying to keep you on *his* side … *but* you don't have to die on the losing side.

> *"Sin can't win. Faith can't fail.*
> *It pays to serve Jesus each day"*
>
> ———————
> (ADRIAN ROGERS).

The devil makes you believe that *Jesus* is just a joke – a myth, a fairy tale, a made-up religious person. This world loves swallowing *that* lie. However, up until 1873, the world said that the ancient city of Troy was just a myth that never existed either. *But* Heinrich Schliemann believed otherwise. So, even though the world laughed and mocked and called him crazy, he persistently kept looking for Troy. Then, in 1873, he miraculously discovered the ancient city of Troy! The battle was over, and the Trojans had triumphed.

May I declare unto you the Truth: *It is finished*, the battle is over, and **"Jesus is LORD!"** Yes!!

Satan screams, "NOOOOO!! *I AM YOUR MASTER!"*

So, the beat goes on ... with you marching to the devil's cadence, and your slave-master driving your soul into a world of turmoil. You're an angry young man ... and you don't know why. *But God* is watching you. He sees your Eternal soul, and *He* knows why. Your soul belongs to satan, and *he* is the one filling it. He has treated you so hatefully for so long that you are as full of hate as he is. And that's why you just sarcastically laugh when people like me tell you that Jesus *Loves* you ... because *your* god hates you and keeps you in a world of hate. You can't begin to imagine a Heavenly Father Who wants to lead you into *His* "World of Love."

So, you exist, but you just can't seem to ever be truly happy ... and you don't know why. I'll tell you why. Satan doesn't *allow* his slaves to be truly happy, that's why. The devil has you in the palm of his grimy hand, and he is squeezing you to death. *Mercy Me!*

Maybe you've tried to escape, but ole slewfoot has a very tight grip on you – his prize slave. Well, take heart, Dear Heart, the Lord Jesus absolutely *Loves* rescuing and redeeming satan's slaves. That fresh air you're breathing is "Jesus" loosening satan's grip on your soul. Praise His Holy Name!

Now, I know what you're thinking, "You're wrong about me. I'm very happy."

Yep, you're about as happy as a spiritually dead person can get. You spend your life serving "number one" – you. May I shock you with the Truth: *GOD,* and God alone, is "Number One" – not *you.* But you live for your own pleasure, not God's. So, *your* pleasure is coming from satan's realm ... from which he allows you a teaspoon of pleasure – then gives you a ton of sorrow to go with it. *And* he has fooled you into believing that this is "just the way life is."

Yep, the life you're living is the best satan can give you, *but* you just haven't tasted "The Best" the Lord Jesus can give you. Your problem is that you have no idea what's on the other side of that door ... if you would dare to open it. That door can only be opened with the hand of Faith ... and Jesus is offering it to you right here, right now. That door is in your heart. You have it bolted against the Lord Jesus. You need to take Jesus' Hand of Faith and open that door. *Now!*

However, I think you know by now who is standing between you and that door. And do you know why satan wants you in hell with him so badly? It's because he's still mad about going there himself. Look around our world. Most people don't want a single desire denied them. Lucifer was the same way in Heaven. He wanted it *all* for himself. *But God* gave him the *opposite* of what he desired – a one-way trip out of Heaven and the loss of everything he desired. And he is *still* seething.

There are many in our world today who, in their hearts, have embraced satan and his evil ways. The more something costs, the more they want it for themselves. They know the price of everything ... and the value of nothing. All they can hear is satan screaming at them, *"You* matter most! So, don't deny yourself *anything* you desire ... even if you have to destroy others to get it – like I did."

But Jesus knows the price of your Salvation and the value of your soul. When you embrace *Him,* He says to you, "*God* matters most! Deny *yourself*. Hold things loosely. Value people! Take up your cross and follow *Me,* and I will make you a fisher of men – like I was."

Let me tell you plainly: *You need the Lord Jesus* to Save you and dwell in your spirit. Then, *He* will give you the desires of

His Heart. You will desire Godly things, and most of all, you will desire *Jesus Himself.*

> *"Delight thyself also in The Lord,*
> *and He shall give thee the desires of thine heart"*
>
> (PSALM 37:4).

Ole slewfoot is lying to you and telling you that you *don't* need the Lord. Nope, you're a "self-made" man. If Abe Lincoln were here, he would say, "I'm glad to hear you say that because it relieves the Creator of a fearful responsibility."

Actually, it's your "god," satan, who takes full responsibility for filling your soul with his demonic pride. Pride keeps you from knowing how lost you are and how helpless you are to save yourself. Only *God* can "Save" you ... *when* you *humble* your soul in the dust and admit to God your sinfulness, helplessness, neediness, and frailty before His Majesty, Holiness, and Glory. But the devil doesn't want you humble. He doesn't want you to know that

> *"a man's pride shall bring him low ...*
> *but honour shall uphold the humble in spirit"*
>
> (PROVERBS 29:23).

> *"Pride forged on the anvil of a hard heart*
> *will escort you to hell"*
>
> (ADRIAN ROGERS).

Satan wants you proud of how intelligent you are. He fools you into trying to *think* your way to God. It will never happen. Salvation is not a mental accomplishment. Salvation is a *Spiritual Transaction* ... between Jesus and you. Salvation is *the Revelation* of Jesus Christ to a lost soul. Salvation occurs when you open your heart's door to Jesus and meet the Crucified Christ *personally*! Salvation is a Supernatural Miracle: The

Holy Blood of God's Son washing all your sins away ... *forever*! Salvation is of the Lord. You aren't Saved by the plan of Salvation ... you are Saved by *The Man* of Salvation, Jesus. That's why a little child can be Saved as easily as a college professor ... or in many cases, even easier, because the Power to be Saved doesn't come from us but from the Lord Himself.

> *"Salvation isn't a gradual reformation.*
> *Salvation is Dynamic Transformation!"*
>
> ———————
> (DAVID JEREMIAH).

So, quit trying to figure God out. He has already figured *you* out, and He knows that you will never reach Him through your "intellectual prowess" – period. C. S. Lewis once said, "Fallen man is not simply an imperfect creature who needs improvement. He is a rebel who must lay down his arms!"

When you finally surrender and lay down your rebellion to the Lord Jesus, He will gladly take you prisoner. But as it is, you're leading "The Resistance Movement" against God! Your marching orders are coming straight from the one who is *presently* holding you prisoner. The devil has you in his clutches, but he doesn't want you to know. So, he makes you think it's all *your* idea to resist Jesus. Satan knows that without Jesus, you will *never* be *spiritually wise*.

The devil loves keeping you proud of your "human intellectual superiority." And I know what your intellect is thinking, "This isn't for me. Nope, being a Christian is just a terrible waste of a life."

Really? Well, if I'm just "wasting" my life on the Lord Jesus Christ and His Eternal Kingdom, then who and what are you wasting *your* life on?

You've got the answer, "I'm not wasting *my* life. I went to college, I read lots of 'enlightened' books and watch the news every night. So, I've got life all figured out, Dude." *(Hmmm)*.

Well, the people who are telling you what to believe don't know that *they* don't know what *they* believe.

They tell you how to live ... when *they* have no "Life" in *them*.

They tell you how to look at life ... when satan has *them* spiritually blind.

They tell you what to think ... when *they* have no knowledge of God.

They tell you what to do ... while *they* just do whatever satan tells *them* to do.

It's time you figured *them* out.

"While they promise them liberty, they themselves are the servants of corruption; for of whom a man is overcome, of the same is he brought into bondage"

(II PETER 2:19).

The Lord wants you to have *true knowledge*, but until you know what you presently *don't* know (God's Truth), you don't know what you don't know — or that you *need* to know what you don't know. What you don't know is that you can never truly know yourself (or the mysteries of life) until you first *know* God. The first step to knowing God is realizing that *He knows you*. And now, you know.

"The liberals say that virtue is for fools"

(RUSH LIMBAUGH).

I will admit that I'm a fool for Jesus. Whose fool are you?

I'm a slave of Christ Jesus. Whose slave are you?

I *know* Whom *I* have believed. Who are you believing?

I serve at the pleasure of my King. Are the gods you're serving bringing you any lasting pleasure?

When you die, will your "life" die with you?

Do you have "a cause" that is *really* worth living for? *Eternally* worth living for?

What is *your* "reason to live"? Mine is the Best Reason in all of time and Eternity – The Eternal King of *all* Creation!

"He is no fool who gives what he cannot keep to gain what he cannot lose"

(JIM ELLIOT).

Satan makes you believe that you can just flip out your smarty-pants phone and find anything you need in this world. Maybe so ... but what about the *next World* – the one that lasts *forever*? To find Eternal Life you must find The One Who *Lives forever* – Jesus Christ. You must meet *Him* personally. And instead of sending you a tweet to your fancy-phone, Jesus sends *His own Spirit* bearing His Glorious Truth into *your very soul*! While you've been chasing after truth, "The Truth" has been closing in on *you*. That's because He knows that your smarty-pants phone won't get you from this world safely into Heaven.

"To believe what God says, to do what God commands, to take that Salvation which God provides ...

this is man's highest and best wisdom"

(CHARLES SPURGEON).

Your "intellectual superiority" tells you that the Bible is just a fairy-tale book. Ah, but you're judging God's Word without realizing that it is God's Word that judges *you*.

So, you say, "I think that all truth is relative."

You're right. All Truth *is* Relative ... a Relative of God – His Son, Jesus Christ! When you die and your spirit-man leaves your Earthsuit, you *will* stand before Him as your Judge. And *that's* the Truth. *Mercy Me!*

However, your intellectual superiority won't give up, so you say, "Let me rephrase my statement. There is *no* absolute truth." *(Hmmm).*

Are you absolutely sure that's absolutely true? If you say "yes," you have just called yourself a liar ... because you have admitted to the existence of at least one absolute truth. And here's some more absolute truth for you: I'm absolutely sure that *I know* The One Who is Faithful and True, and *His Word* is "Absolute Truth!"

Truth is, it's time for you to challenge your intellect by reading, researching and studying "The Book of the Ages." Then, challenge your integrity by honestly drawing the conclusion that the Bible is indeed a *Supernatural Book*. There are amazing messages encrypted into the Scriptures that, once uncovered by Bible Scholars, can only by explained one way: A Supernatural God did it!

Adrian Rogers says that many a man has preached the funeral for the Bible, but their only problem is that the corpse has out-lived the pallbearers! The Anvil of the Truth of God's Word has worn out many a hammer. So, perhaps it's time you resigned your job as a pallbearer of the Bible.

God says that His Word (the Bible) is "Alive!" It is also powerful and sharper than any two-edged sword (Hebrews 4:12). Get yourself a Bible, read the Gospels about Jesus (the Son of God) and find out for yourself. As you read, the Truth of God's Word and the Power of His Holy Spirit will pierce your dark soul, enter your dead spirit and make *you* "Alive!" too. You'll see.

Now, you may be the person who is just laughing your way through all of this so far ... because *you* have totally given yourself over to the devil, joined his "church" and have become his devout worshiper. You proudly bear the name of your master. You're a "satanist" ... in covenant with the devil himself! You have an insatiable desire for the salacious – lusts given to you by your satanic master. The more of satan's sordid self he fills you with, the easier it gets for you to make his evil sacrifices and act out his perverted wickedness. The more of your soul you give to him, the more of his demonic power he gives to you. You are reigning *on Earth* with satan – deliriously dancing with demons. You have a fatal attraction to *the very one* who has sealed your eternal death sentence!

The devil doesn't care anything about your *Eternal soul*. He hates you and is gleefully destroying you. Sadly, the *Joy* of Jesus and the comfort of His *Love* are completely foreign to you. Instead, you are drunk with the wine of satan's wickedness. *But* a sobering day *is* coming. It's called "the moment of your death." That's when you discover what a fool you've been. Satan has just been playing you, because *now* he has *no* power to deliver you from eternal damnation in hell. *Mercy Me!*

As I stand securely in Christ, and Christ alone, and look out over the landscape of this wicked world, I can "see" that being a leader in satan's evil kingdom is highly over-rated. In fact … it's less than nothing.

Are you still reading? Good, because now things are going to start looking up … literally.

The God of your Salvation has much better things for you than what satan has been dragging you through. And deep in your heart, God's Son is slowly but surely dawning.

However, the prince of darkness doesn't want you to know that there really *is* a Supreme, Supernatural Being of such Wisdom, Power, Intellect, Knowledge, Ability, Creativity, Love, Joy, and Grace that we can't even begin to fathom Him with our mortal minds. And yet, we *all* live and have our being in His Glorious Presence!

> *"Holy, Holy, Holy, is The Lord Almighty;*
> *the whole Earth is full of His Glory!"*
>
> (ISAIAH 6:3).

Ole slewfoot doesn't want you to know that Almighty God is the One Who kicked him out of Heaven for his rebellion (ever wondered why you're such a rebel?), and he landed on Planet Earth. That ole devil is now out of a job, but he doesn't like his retirement plan. So, he has been on the war-path for vengeance ever since. That is why there is such chaos in our world. (America is a Nation in rebellion against God, because satan is "the god of this world.") And that is also why there is such chaos in your own soul. You were born into this world with satan's seed of rebellion imbedded in your heart.

"I saw a parking place the other day with a sign: 'Don't even think about parking here!' And I was so full of rebellion ... that I actually thought about it"

(ADRIAN ROGERS).

The master liar is frantically trying to keep the Truth from you, *but God* has out-maneuvered ole slewfoot by getting me to you with the Truth that there really *is* a True and Living God – Creator of Heaven and Earth. And get this, Creator of *you*!

Oh no! Satan wants you to keep on believing his ridiculous, made-up evil lie he calls "evolution." Now do you *really* believe you're a monkey's uncle ... or rather, that a monkey is *your* uncle?

Of course, he isn't. *God* is your Creator! Maybe you don't believe in God (yet), but let me assure you, He believes in *you* – *He Created* you (along with everything else). You were fearfully and wonderfully *Created* by the God Who *Loves* you.

"The Spirit of God hath made me, and the Breath of The Almighty hath given me life!"

(JOB 33:4).

The reason people don't believe in the Miracle Birth of Jesus is because they don't believe in *their own* "miracle birth." *All* of life is a Miracle! Your earthly life is a Miracle from beginning to end. Have you ever considered the fact that you spent the first nine months of your life under water – *and you didn't drown!*? You were miraculously designed, engineered, and formed – cell by cell, molecule by molecule – as you were amazingly created in the womb of your mother. And you're telling me that senseless, powerless "evolution" did it all. For pity's sake, don't insult our Infinitely Wise, Gloriously Powerful Heavenly Father by saying such a ridiculous thing! He's listening, you know, and writing it *all* down … for later.

Jesus' earthly Life was also one continuous Miracle (from a virgin's womb filled to a burial tomb sealed – then miraculously emptied)! Our Great God created *everything* out of "nothing." So, tell me again how a God *that* Powerful can't control an egg in a virgin's womb that *He* created. Right.

God is Powerful enough to fill the entire Universe, as well as be contained in the Son of a woman … for with God nothing shall be impossible (Luke 1:37). Jesus often called Himself "The Son of Man." He became The Son of Man that *we* might become the sons of God. Hallelujah!

(**NOTE**: When we say that God creates out of nothing, we mean that He creates out of things we can't see. However, quantum physics is now revealing to us that "nothing" isn't really nothing. Nope, it's actually *"God's* Nothing." Some of the scientists who discovered quantum mechanics are admitting that even *they* don't really understand it. How 'bout that. Man is being forced to bow to an Intelligence and Power greater than himself after all. "If you think you understand quantum mechanics, you don't understand quantum mechanics" {Dr. Richard Feynman}.)

God is way too marvelously *Supernatural* for us mere mortals to understand Him. If you are looking for a god you can totally understand, stay away from the True and Living God. Until you realize how *Supernatural* your own birth and life are, you will never be able to fathom our Great God. It took a Super Intelligent, Super Creative, Super Wise, Super Powerful, Supernatural Being to *Create* (from *another dimension*) everything we can see and can't see. The reason young people are wondering if they are a boy or a girl these days is because they don't know that *"God* Created" them in the first place. When you know Whose you are ... you will *know* who you are.

America has lost her identity as a Christian Nation; therefore, her citizens are losing *their* identity as Christians. When I was coming along, we didn't have any trouble telling who the men were and who the women were. God made it perfectly evident – and He still does.

If our Grandparents could come back today, they would declare they had landed on the wrong planet! *But*, as soon as they realized (along with Pogo the Possum) that they has met the enemy, and he r *us* ... we would get the switching of our lives! That's because *they* didn't trash the Bible *or* the God of the Bible (like the liberals do today), *and* they didn't *allow* anyone else to either.

In their day, *we* were disciplined and made to "walk a straight line." Too many people today are following the crooked path of that ole serpent, satan. If *we* had tried the shenanigans being done these days, they would have sent *us* to "the funny farm." *Mercy Me!*

However, in *modern* America, you must totally and wholeheartedly embrace any and every *sin* known to man (and a few they have recently invented) lest you be accused of being an insensitive person who callously hurts other people's feelings. Well, our Grandparents didn't mind hurting *our* feelings (along with a few of our body parts) in order to put "the fear of God" in us. The reason they did it was because *they* feared God themselves. It would be a wonderful thing if they *could* come back today ... because we could sure use them to "Make America Godly Again!"

The Pilgrims who came over on the Mayflower were all Christians. They said that they came here "for the Glory of

God and the advancement of the Christian Faith," and so, they founded *Christian* Colonies.

Today, however, Christianity has been rejected and replaced with "the religion of the day" – humanism. Man is now "god," and *he* creates his own reality (Rush calls it "an alternative universe") in which *he* decides which sex he wants to be ... instead of gladly accepting the Truth that *God Created* him the sex *He* wants him to be. In the humanist's mind, God has no right to tell man which sex he is. Nope, it's *man's* job to tell *God* which sex he is ... *and* tell God which sex *He* is. Amazing! Sounds to me like they've all swallowed the same fruity lie Eve did back in The Garden ... and today, the inmates are running the asylum.

Yep, there is still a crooked devil living in a crooked universe at the end of a crooked path, and plenty of folks are following him these days. He keeps them blinded to the fact that it doesn't matter if you're politically on the Right or on the Left ... when you die, you're *still* going either UP, or you're going down. In the final analysis, it won't matter where you stood politically on this Earth. In "The Final Analysis," it will only matter where you are standing *Spiritually* as you stand before The King of this Universe, Jesus Christ! So, get right with Him, or be left by Him.

People are sorely disoriented today because they refuse to follow the *True North Star* – the Lord Jesus. They reject the *Miraculous Power* He possesses and the *Glorious Grace* He bestows. When you bow your knee to Him, the Light of the World leads you into all Truth.

"From the beginning of **The Creation***, GOD made them male and female. For this cause shall a man leave his father and mother, and shall cleave to his wife."*
Signed: Jesus

(MARK 10:6-7).

There is certainly enough obvious God-given evidence proving which sex you are that all you have to do to find out which sex you are is just go look in a mirror (or ask your Grandparents). And there is so much reliable scientific data proving the impossibility of evolution that it makes you wonder why a truly intelligent person would profess to believe it. You can prove that evolution is just "fake news" the same way you proved which sex you are – just go look in a mirror (or ask your Grandparents).

I dare you to do an in-depth study of your "Miraculously Created" human body and learn how every amazing part works together (the brain, the heart, the liver, the blood, the bones, the eyes, the male/female reproductive systems, etc.) and how every single cell works individually (like little factories), and then tell me that it all just *somehow* "evolved" out of dead matter without any Supernatural Intelligence or Power involved whatsoever ... and say it with a straight face. Read Dr. Richard Swenson's book *More Than Meets the Eye* and let God's Truth open *your* eyes. And besides, if evolution were really true, then how come Mothers still only have two hands?

Open your mind, open your eyes and look around this world. Now, how did the millions upon millions of different people, animals, reptiles, insects, trees, flowers, vegetables, and weeds all decide *on their own* what they wanted to be, and *then* miraculously *create themselves* from non-living matter? If a camera can't *create itself,* then how could your miraculously complex eye have ever created *itself*? If a computer can't *create itself,* then how could your miraculously complex brain have ever created *itself*?

Oh, I see – it just takes a long time.

Wake up! Shake off satan's shackles! It couldn't happen in a million years ... in a billion years ... in a quadrillion years! It *DIDN'T* happen!! If you truly believe that dead matter just *somehow* gave "life" to itself, and eventually "just happened" to *turn itself* into a *Miraculous Human Being* ... well ... maybe a monkey really *is* your uncle after all.

In a powerfully *miraculous*, amazingly *creative* way, the Lord places an *astronomical* amount of Super-Intelligent Information into the DNA of every living cell, along with His Divinely controlled *Energy* ... and the poor evolutionists don't know how it gets there or where it comes from. It takes *conscious* "Intelligent Energy" to create *order*. Without it, you only have *chaos*. If you doubt me, just go take a look at your teenager's room. Now, if by some *miracle* it's in order, you will know for sure: "There has to be a God!"

Worldlings insist on saying, "Where is God? We can't see Him – so He doesn't exist."

Well, they need look no farther than me. Not only did God *Himself* create me (spirit, soul, body) and give me life, but He also gave me *Eternal Life* by "Saving" my Eternal soul. Then, He totally transformed my life and gloriously "Lives" in me today. Born-Again Christians are the most amazingly convincing proof of God on this Earth!

The Bible tells us that lots of folks believed in Jesus when they saw the Miracles He performed. Well, here I am – a *Miracle* of God! And *you* will stand judged before Him one day for witnessing His Miracle ... then turning away in unbelief.

The "Voice" you are hearing is *God* ... giving you the opportunity to change your mind, your heart, your will ... your Destiny! Jesus Himself is offering you a new set of eyes – *Spiritual Eyes*! He wants you to "see" His Miracle Creations *and* His Miracle Re-Creations: Born-Again Christians.

> *"Thou art worthy, O Lord,*
> *to receive Glory and Honor and Power;*
> *for Thou hast Created all things!"*

OLE SLEWFOOT

Hallelujah!

(REVELATION 4:11).

I don't know about you, but I don't want the man-god/no-god of the evolutionists/atheists. I want my God – the Almighty Supernatural God of all Creation! Until a man admits that all science (so-called) is simply the study of our Creator God, he is woefully "unwise" ... no matter how many plaques he may have on his wall. God's Awesome Supernatural Fingerprints are undeniably on every molecule of His Created Universe!

"We have educated ourselves into fools.
We have been duped by satan
into letting science steal God from us"

(TONY EVANS).

"When you study DNA, it cries out,
'In the beginning, God Created ... !'"

(KEN HAM).

The only reason you believe in false evolution is because you *refuse* to believe in the One True God – the God *you* can't understand. You want a god you can "figure out." So, you invent your own god ... who is no smarter than you are. Can't I interest you in a God Who is a whole lot smarter than *that*?

To find *God's Truth*, look into the excellent ministries: "Answers in Genesis" and "Institute for Creation Research" for a start (and while you're there, check out "global warming"). But you don't really need science to prove to you that you live in a "Divinely Miraculous World." You are a miraculously complex person who was created by a "Personal, Miracle-working God." If you can read John Ashton's book *Evolution Impossible,* and still claim to believe in evolution ... well ... you probably don't know which sex you are either.

MOLLY MCCOY

"Earth's crammed with Heaven,
And every common bush afire with God;
But only he who sees, takes off his shoes,
The rest sit around and pluck blackberries."

(ELIZABETH BARRETT BROWNING)

"For the invisible things of (God) from the *Creation* of the World are clearly seen, being understood by the things that are made, even His Eternal Power and Godhead; so that they are without excuse" (Romans 1:20). And *you,* my Friend, are without excuse also. When you stand before God in judgment and try to explain why you didn't believe in Him, He's just going to laugh – and *you* are going to cry. On the other hand, you *could* become His Dear Child and one day stand before Him with great joy – the Joy of Jesus!

"I can see how it might be possible for a man to look down
upon Earth and be an atheist, but I cannot conceive how he
could look up into the heavens and say there is no God!"

(ABRAHAM LINCOLN).

Truth is, evolution is just the "religion" of the atheists. So why, pray tell, are they allowed to teach it in our public schools, for pity's sake? Why haven't the "religion police" shown up with their lawyers?

Answer: Because ole slewfoot has shown up with his lies ... in order to keep this world (and you) in his clutches! Aren't you tired of being satan's beat-up, spiritually starved POW? Wouldn't you just love to know "The Way" of escape from satan's prison? Just asking.

OLE SLEWFOOT

Ole wardenfoot has you doing time in his dismal jail with barred windows, so you can't see that "Love" is at the Heart of our Universe. The God Who created it *all* is the God of Love! God created you, and He Loves you with an Everlasting Love that satan wishes he could destroy – but he can't. The devil can't destroy God or His Great Love for you, but the deceiver *can* blind the eyes of your heart to God's Truth ... and he's been doing a mighty good job of that in *your* life so far. However, the Hounds of Heaven are on your trail ... sent by the God Who Loves you!

The "demon-god of this world" doesn't want you to know that the True God, in His Love and Mercy, has provided *The Lamb,* Jesus, Who offers you *The Way* to be rescued from satan's clutches and delivered out of his evil kingdom of death. I'm sure you've seen pictures of Jesus on the Cross. Have you ever wondered why so many people make such a big deal out of a Man dying on a Cross? If you have never heard the Gospel of Jesus Christ, you are about to hear the best "Breaking News" you've ever heard!

First, do you remember the worst *broken news*? Yep, sin has broken your fellowship with God and separated you from your Creator. So, how can your sin be blotted out? Good news! Your *Eternal Salvation* is possible today because 2,000 years ago God's Son came *Himself* to this Earth He created and went to a cruel Roman Cross to hang there and die there ... to pay the penalty for all *your* sin! (Even though you may not believe that {yet}, it's *still true.*)

"For as by one man's disobedience many were made sinners,
so by the obedience of One shall many be made Righteous ...
even so might Grace reign through Righteousness
unto Eternal Life by Jesus Christ our Lord"

(ROMANS 5:19, 21).

The demonic prince of darkness is hoping you never hear

God's Truth, but I'm going to tell you anyway. When Jesus, God's Son, was hanging on that Cross dying for the sins of the whole world ... He was thinking ... about *you*! And He's *still* thinking about you.

"I AM the Good Shepherd,
and know My Sheep, and am known of Mine."
Signed: Jesus

(JOHN 10:14).

Satan hates me for telling you this because he knows it's true: **Jesus Loves You!** And Jesus' Love for you is *stronger* than all the hate the devil can bring up out of hell. The Son of God has set His Heart on you ... *YOU*! Jesus wants *your* heart for His very own. He will never stop pursuing you with His Love. And yet, Jesus is a Gentleman. He makes His Love known to you, then waits for you to respond ... to *Him*.

Even though Jesus has overcome the world (John 16:33), He has never overcome *you* (up until now). He waits patiently for you to throw out your pride, humble yourself before God, confess your sin to Him, admit your need of Him and yield to God's rule over you. Then, Jesus will enter in, claim you for His very own and set satan's slave free indeed – for good!

However, the evil one *presently* overcoming you doesn't want you knowing that the Blood flowing from Jesus' body on that Cross is the Precious, Holy Blood of God ... being spilled out for *you*! Nor does satan want you believing that Jesus dying on the Cross is *God Loving you*! God's great Love, Mercy, Grace, and Forgiveness are *all* being poured out for *you* ... through Jesus, His Son.

"Behold, the Lamb of God
Who taketh away the sin of the world (and you!)"

(JOHN 1:29).

Worthy is The Lamb Who was slain! Holy is Thy Name. All Praise to "The King of kings!" The Lamb upon that Cross is The King within my heart! But satan sure doesn't want Jesus to be *your* King. So, he's blinding you to the Radiant Glory of God's Son – the One on that Cross giving His Life for you. Thus, ole slewfoot keeps you from ever thinking about how Holy and Righteous Jesus is ... and how evil and wicked you are. The devil doesn't want you to know the Truth: It should be *you* on that Cross ... *but Jesus,* God's Son, is taking *your* place! Jesus is worthy! You and I are worthy too ... of judgment.

However, you think that life is all about *you,* don't you? You're so vain. "God is up to something much bigger than just you" (Tony Evans). Right, and it's *JESUS*! The One big enough to rule the Universe was small enough to become a humble Servant ... all the way to Calvary's Cross. Jesus' Kingdom is the only kingdom ever established by the death of its King. The Love of God, the *Humility* of Jesus, and the Power of His Spirit are forever *Victorious* over evil satan – the leader of the "human pride parade."

Have you ever heard of "Calvary Love"? Well, I'll tell you about it. *Calvary Love* goes to a cruel wooden Roman Cross to agonize, suffer and die there for people who hate You. *Calvary Love* forgives the ones who beat Your back, hit You in the face, drive the nails, pull out Your beard and crush the crown of thorns down upon Your precious head. *Calvary Love* sacrifices and gives *to the death* for those who curse You, mock You and spit upon You. *Calvary Love* gives it's last breath to deliver from hell those who have put You through it.

At *this moment,* God has drawn you to the foot of His Son's Cross to reveal to you His Great Love for you ... even if Jesus Christ is your favorite curse word. And why does Jesus Love you so? I'll tell you why ... just because He Loves you so. If you can't figure that out, don't worry, you're not alone. None of us can – but we don't turn it down ... and neither should you. The

Lord Jesus wants to teach you all about "Calvary Love." And then ... He wants to fill you with it. Let Him.

> *"But God commendeth His Love toward us, in that,*
> *while we were yet sinners, Christ died for us"*
>
> (ROMANS 5:8).

Ole slewfoot doesn't want you to linger at the foot of Jesus' Cross for very long. He's afraid you might hear Jesus calling your name (John 10:3). Horrors! The enemy of your soul is desperately trying to keep this Truth from you: Jesus knows *you*! There's a good chance that your parents didn't plan you. *But God* did! There's even a chance that you don't know who your real father is. But I know Who your Real Father *could be*. He's The One Who knows who you are and where you are. God knows everything you've ever thought, everything you've ever said, and everything you've ever done or even thought about doing. Scary, isn't it? Good, you need to be scared ... but not afraid to keep reading. Keep pressing on, and you shall know the Truth and the One Who *is* the Truth ... and *He* will set you free!

The God Who created you watches your every move. He *sees* your prideful, arrogant, rebellious heart. He hears *every* word that crosses your lips (yep, even *those)*. He knows your innermost thoughts that set *fire* to your soul! And He is writing it all down in His Book. You will see it again. After death comes "Judgment!" You laugh. But just remember: He Who laughs last, laughs loudest.

However, God won't be laughing when He condemns you to an Eternity separated from His Presence and His Holy Heaven

... and neither will you.

*"You can laugh your way into hell,
but you can't laugh your way out once you get there!"*

(ADRIAN ROGERS).

And you can't buy your way out either – your money will all be long gone.

You will wish with every fiber of your being and every ounce of your soul that you had listened when Christians tried to warn you of your *ultimate fate*. You will finally *know* that they were telling you *the Truth*, but you willingly chose to believe satan's lies instead. The Truth is, God is the God of *Eternal Love* ... to those who *respond* to His Love. To those who spend their life *spurning* His Love, He will give them their wish – He will spurn *them* for all Eternity. *Mercy Me!*

So, all you God-haters out there can relax. The day *is* coming when you will finally be completely and totally free of God – separated from Him in torturous black darkness and utter aloneness (except for the demons surrounding you). Never again will you have to worry about being confronted by a Christian ... *or* the Lord Jesus Who Lives in them. The Saviour's nail-pierced Hand will no longer be extended to *you*. And you will finally be done with God – *forever*! (But you won't like it.)

While we Christians are enjoying Heaven's Bliss, *you* will be in hellish torment – *forever*! Just remember: It's what you wanted. You will finally get what you want, but you won't want what you get. Satan makes you want what he has to offer so badly that you can't see God's Truth for his lies.

The final words of Sir ~~Walter~~ Thomas Scott were these:

"Until this moment, I thought there was neither a God nor a hell. Now, I know that there are both, and I am doomed to perdition by the just judgment of The Almighty!"

Do you feel doomed? Are you stuck in a rut and can't get out? Bad news: You don't have the strength to crawl out by yourself. You will just totally wear yourself out without ever getting out ... *unless* Someone Else stronger than you reaches down and lifts you out of your pit.

Good news! Someone is here to do just that – *If* you will look to Him and *let* Him. *This* is your "Lazarus Moment." When he was lying stone-cold dead in a tomb, Jesus called out, "Lazarus, come forth!" And Lazarus came forth ... to *new life*.

Dear Heart, *listen*! This book is "Jesus" calling out to spiritually dead *you* to come unto *Him* for "New Life in Christ!" So, listen with your heart ... and then respond to "Jesus' Call." He's calling you *by your name*!

> *"My Sheep hear My Voice, and I know them,*
> *and they follow Me."*
> *Signed: Jesus*
> _____
> (JOHN 10:27).

In our world today, there are Christians and there are atheists (lots of 'em). The anti-God people love to ridicule us, mock us, curse us and laugh at us. But they need to stop and consider this. It has been said: God made big men, and God made little men ... and Mr. Colt made the equalizer. But truer still: God made big men, and God made little men ... *and God* made the equalizer: **DEATH!**

The anti-God people who don't believe in God and mock God (even curse God) are hoping with all their heart and soul that they are right ... because they know that *if they are wrong*, when they die they are going to be in very *Big Trouble* with a very *Big God* – Who is going to condemn them to *Eternal* banishment from Him!

"If you say 'No!' to the God of Love and Grace now, the 'Day' is coming when the God of Judgment will say 'No!' to you"

(ADRIAN ROGERS).

In a Divinely Supernatural way, Jesus is dying on the Cross to pay the penalty for the sins of everyone in the world ... and the world doesn't care. They are spiritually dead in their trespasses and sins (like you). Jesus is giving His Divine Life for them, for pity's sake! JESUS CARES!! But they couldn't care less. Belonging to Jesus just isn't in vogue right now. Belonging to satan is *so cool* ... right now. But what a difference a death makes. *Then*, belonging to satan is microwave hot!

"The God in Whose Hand thy breath is hast thou not Glorified"

(DANIEL 5:23).

If I have just described you, don't wait until you die to find out how wrong you are. You are in *Big Trouble* ... *NOW*! The liar who is telling you how right you are is making an Eternal fool out of you. *For Once in Your Life* wise-up and listen to the God of this Universe speaking His Truth to your soul! He *Loves* you. The evil one you are following *hates* you. Keep on down his road, and one day you will find out just how much.

Truth is, death isn't a permanent sleep. Oh no, death is the final "Awakening!" Satan doesn't want you to know that the end of your existence on Planet Earth is *not* the end of your existence. You will still exist ... somewhere. When you come to the end of your life, you will be just moments away from experiencing the reality of that Truth. The road you *choose* to take through this life will determine, no doubt, which way you go at *that moment*. Don't take the low road. You won't find Jesus on it. It's time you chose a new path in life because you are always a lot closer to falling off the edge of Eternity than you could ever possibly imagine! There is but a heartbeat between you and *eternal* death.

> *"Life isn't over when it's over.*
> *On the other side of your last heartbeat is Eternity!"*
>
> (CHARLES STANLEY).

Every funeral is a celebration. If the person whose remains are in the casket was a Born-Again Christian, all of Heaven and the people who knew them are celebrating! *But*, if the person was a rebel who *rejected Jesus* as their Saviour right down to their last breath … all of *hell* is celebrating. *Mercy Me!*

This entire book is "Jesus" pouring His Heart out to you and promising that if you will just open *your heart* up to Him, *He Will Come In*. Really! Jesus is pleading with you, "Please, *let Me* touch you and enter into your heart while I AM so near to you. I AM God's Son, and I want to come into your spirit and give you 'Life!' Then, I will use you mightily as My Ambassador on Earth and one day take you Home to Heaven to be with Me and all My saints – *forever*! Listen to My Voice as I unfold to you "The Way" for *you* to become My Disciple whom I Love."

> *"We are Ambassadors for Christ,*
> *as though God did beseech you by us:*
> *We pray you in Christ's stead, be ye reconciled to God!"*
>
> (II CORINTHIANS 5:20).

However … if you're convinced that everything *satan* is telling you is true, then just go ahead and curse, smoke, drink, do drugs, live loose, and party ... Party ... PARTEEE!! Hurt others at will, kill whomever you choose, steal whatever you want (sound like our riots?) because there is nothing after death to even be concerned about. Nothing matters. Just waste your life ... because it's all just a big waste anyway. Right? (satan says "Right!")

However ... if *God* is "Right" and there really *is* "Life" after death, then you had better wake up *now* and consider some things. Your flesh-man is having a blast ... as long as your Earthsuit lasts. *But,* there is coming a day when the storm clouds shall rise ... and your Earthman *will* fall. Then, your *spirit-man* will rise out of your dead-man and go to God's judgment. You will be judged for every moment you lived on Planet Earth. So, you may be controlling things pretty well right now, but after the death of your Earthsuit, you won't have that luxury. This is literally a matter of life or death – Eternal **Life** ... or eternal **death**!

Satan keeps you looking for "life" in all the wrong places – parties, drugs, sex, money, fame, power ... *anything* to keep you from looking unto Jesus – the One Who has the Power to give you *real life – Spiritual Life*! You, my Friend, can be an *ultimate winner* and live with King Jesus for *all Eternity*! But *not* if you stay in loser satan's evil kingdom of death.

The choice is yours alone. You can continue living in satan's kingdom and letting him devilishly control your desires and lusts so that you end up living like an animal, *or* you can live in Jesus' Kingdom and let *Him* Divinely control your soul and body so that you end up living like your Glorious Lord. Up until now, you have spent your whole life thinking and living on "the animal level." But *now,* it's time for you to let the God of this Universe take you up to *His* level – the Heavenly level! *Then,* He will use you as a *major player* in His Eternal Kingdom ... as soon as you are ready.

Now, I know what you're thinking, "I'm not a Christian, but I certainly don't live on the animal level, for pity's sake!"

Well, I would be willing to wager my next Social Security check that you not only live on the animal level, but you also live on the devil's level.

"You're on!"

Yep, I'm on alright ... to you. I know that you have various and sundry conversations with yourself that sound something like this: "Am I happy? Am I *really* happy? Am I fulfilled and completely satisfied with everything in my life ... and *everyone* in my life? Has life treated me fair? Have I gotten everything I deserve in life? Do I deserve more? Do I deserve better? Of course, I do! I deserve better than I've got. I deserve more than I've got. I deserve *THAT* ... bathing herself down there before my eyes. *That's* what *I* deserve. That's what I want, and that's what I'm gonna get ... *NOW*! No matter the cost! (II Samuel 11).

(I don't know every little thing you've ever lusted after and stepped on everyone around you to get ... I just know that you have had your share of "Bathshebas" in your life.)

Now, can you think of anyone else who had a similar conversation with himself once upon a time in Heaven ... just before God kicked him out? And you don't think you live on the devil's level... I rest my case (and you owe me).

"Ye are of your father the devil,
and the lusts of your father ye will do." Signed: Jesus

(JOHN 8:44).

My Friend, you have a major dilemma: You have a huge hole in your soul. And you know it ... because you've been stuffing everything imaginable on this Earth into that hole trying to fill it up and give you some satisfaction – but to no avail. Right? Of course. But you may as well just give up. Nothing on God's green Earth will ever satisfy you. There's not a possession, a position, or a power that will ever do it. There's not a person on the face of this Earth who can give you the "love" you are longing for ... and need.

You are desperately trying to fill a spiritual void with physical things. You will never succeed. You're stuffing physical stuff into your spiritual soul and wondering why it doesn't work.

"Why do I *still* feel so empty?"

I know your frustration. For many years, I was just like you ... *until* I met the only One Who is big enough to fill my heart, my soul, and my spirit with His Divine Self! You see, *God* is the One Who has engineered your dilemma of being unhappy and discontent with *everything* ... so that you will seek "The One True Source" of real joy and contentment.

You have a Jesus-shaped vacuum in your soul, and only *He* can fill it. The Lord Jesus is looking straight at you and asking, "Are you finally ready to let *Me* in?"

So, are you?

"Be strong and of good courage and do it!"

(I CHRONICLES 28:20).

"I don't know your problem today. I don't know your need, but I do know your Answer ... and His Name is Jesus"

(ADRIAN ROGERS).

The Lord Jesus is presently with you in all of His Glory! You don't believe that ... because you can't see Him. But that doesn't move Him. He is *still* there – watching you.

"And I, John, turned to see ... One like unto The Son of Man ... and His Eyes were as a flame of fire!"

(REVELATION 1:12-14).

You can't touch Jesus – physically. *But Jesus* can touch *you* – spiritually. *And you* can touch *Him* – spiritually. Amazing! The Spiritual Blood of Jesus Christ being shed for you on His Eternal Cross has the Power to "Save" your Eternal soul. When you touch Jesus with a heart of Faith, He touches *you* with His powerful Spiritual Hands and applies His Blood (representing His death for you) to your inner spirit-man.

However, right now, you may feel like His Hands are twisting your mind into a "spiritual pretzel." You may even feel like you're losing your mind. *But Jesus* knows that you are just coming to your senses ... at last. He knows that things aren't really falling apart in your life; they are just falling into place ... finally. And He should know – *He* is the One doing it *all*.

So, just keep reading, and Christ's Spirit will keep removing the scales from your spiritual eyes ... until you "see" Jesus, God's Son. Then, God's Spirit will start softening your hard heart and turning it toward Jesus ... until you *want Him* to be *your* Saviour. The moment you do, and touch Him in Faith, is the moment He touches *you* with His Redeeming Blood – "the Price" required for Him to purchase you from satan's slave-block.

People are always marching through our streets demanding

"justice." Well, don't ever march up to *God* and demand justice. If God gives you justice, you will end up in hell ... because that's what you (and all the rest of us) deserve. What you desperately need is God's *Mercy*. You need for God to withhold from you that which you so justly deserve. And when you humbly ask God for His Mercy, He smiles and bestows His Grace on you as well. God's Grace gives you what you need but in no way deserve.

When you cling to Faith alone in Christ alone through Grace alone and give God your sin, He gives you His Son's death ... *and* His Son's *Life*! Then, God clings to *you* as closely as He clings to His Son, Jesus. Wow! That's when you discover that "Jesus is *enough*."

Are you eager to see *all* that Jesus has for you? Well, buckle your seat belt!

However, you're saying, "I don't have time for Jesus right now ... I'm on my way to *The TOP*!"

Yeah, right. And we'll be seeing you again ... on your way down. Without the Lord Jesus, you're headed for the bottom. You will just spend your life working your way *down* the ladder of success.

> *"I met God on my way up.*
> *I got to know Him on my way down"*
>
> ---
>
> (DAVE RAMSEY).

Every day, the world rolls over onto someone who was sitting on top of it the day before. Without Jesus, you're just a sitting duck – for satan. Ole slewfoot loves to keep you risking everything performing for *him* in his "Big Shot Show." But if you don't find yourself a new "life's calling" pretty soon, satan's gonna have to find himself a new stunt man. *Mercy Me!*

Ole slewfoot wants you to keep looking for your life's calling in the yellow pages. He sure doesn't want you looking in the pages of the Bible instead. But why not spite the devil and read Jesus' powerful Words *out loud* ... since *Jesus* is the One "calling" you.

You'll read in John 15:16, Jesus' words: "I have chosen you." How cool is that? Can you imagine the God of this Universe picking you out and choosing *you*? I know that Jesus chose *me*. *Now* He's speaking those words directly to *you*. Could it be that He chose *you* from the foundation of the world ... the same way He chose me?

First, Jesus chooses you, and then it's your turn to choose Him. When you choose Jesus as your Saviour, He will choose to use you so amazingly that you will say, "Yes! I was made for *this*! Jesus chose me for *this very moment*!"

So, choose ye this day whom you will serve – the Lord Jesus or satan. Make up your mind. Do you want all that God is waiting to give you *or* what satan has been giving you all your life? Before you decide, take the "long look" into Eternity. Destiny's door turns on very small hinges. One little decision from you may seem to be just a small thing. *But*, when you choose to choose Jesus, the most important thing you will ever do in your whole life has just been done! *You* make the choice – *He* provides the Power. There's Power in the Precious Blood of Jesus! So, don't just sit there ... *choose*!

Maybe you're choosing not to choose Jesus. You're saying, "Me ... I just leave God alone, and He leaves me alone."

Oh, you think so? Well, who do you think is the One Who gives you *life*? Or a world to live in, a mind to think with, a heart to love with, people to love, and people who love you? Who do you think is the One Who is speaking to your heart right now? If you say "no one," I'm not going to stand next to you in a lightning storm. You know better. You can't get away from God (and His Voice) no matter how fast you run or how far you travel. God's Love and Mercy can out-run you any day of the week. And He is a lot closer to you than you think. *Mercy Me!*

So, quit running, for pity's sake! Aren't you totally worn-out yet? When you finally get to where you're headed, where will you be? Aren't you ever so tired of living in the far country? Aren't you tired of feeling like a motherless child a long way from Home? Aren't you homesick for Heaven? Aren't you finally ready to cry "Uncle!" and cry out to God,

"O wretched man that I am!
Who shall deliver me from the body of this death?"

(ROMANS 7:24).

You're running from The One you need to turn and embrace ... in your heart. Lonely people aren't really lonely – they're just empty. *But Jesus* is more than ready to fill your soul *full to overflowing* with His Glorious Self. And trust me, Jesus is a lot *Bigger* than whatever is the matter at the moment.

Ask yourself this question, "Who am I following?" In the depths of your soul, you're following *someone;* and you will end up where they end up. Your choices are: The Ultimate Winner ... or the judged, condemned loser. You are dying even as you die in "satan's house of the rising sin." However, you *could be* truly "living!" as you live in "Jesus' Kingdom of The Risen Son."

Please, for a Mother's sake and for Jesus' sake, don't let ole slewfoot be your ruin. Let *the Lord* be your Redemption! Then you'll know how much better it is to belong to King Jesus than to be a slave on satan's chain gang. The devil is *not* an e.o.s.m. (equal opportunity slave master). Nope, he exerts all of his demonic power over you to keep you working only for *him* in his evil kingdom – pushing his wicked agenda. But he greatly underestimates his Competition: King Jesus – Who has Supreme Power over *him.* And Jesus *is* an E.O.S. (Equal Opportunity Saviour)!

Now, maybe you've already made it to the top and you're saying, "I'm very well off. I've got everything and have need of nothing."

Yep, you've got everything alright ... except the *one thing* you really do need – the One Who gave you everything in the first place! A wise man once said that *true joy* is not having much to live on – but much to live for.

"Charge them that are rich in this world, that they be not high-minded, nor trust in uncertain riches, but in the Living God, Who giveth us richly all things to enjoy"

(I TIMOTHY 6:17).

Don't be an atheist who enjoys myriads of God's wonderful Blessings ... but has no one to thank for them.

Maybe you *are* an atheist, and you're saying, "My Mother got cancer, and I tried praying to God that He would heal her ... but she died. So, there's no God." *(Hmmm)*.

Well, if God doesn't really exist, then why are we even having this conversation? Why not have a conversation with *yourself* about the deep, heart-felt love you *still* have for your Mother. But, alas, that presents a problem, doesn't it ... because when you rejected God, you also rejected love. The rock-solid Truth of this Universe is: God is Love. So, if you have no God, then you have no love either. Therefore, what is your complaint?

Of course, God exists! And He isn't going to cease to exist simply because you choose to "say" that you don't believe in Him. Truth is, your *true heart* knows that your mouth is lying ...

because God speaks to everyone of us deep in our heart when our Earthman isn't looking. *Mercy Me!*

Let me say that I surely know your sorrow of losing someone you dearly love, and my heart goes out to you. I also know that our God is a Good God Who has a reason and a purpose for *everything* He does ... whether we understand it, or not. God sees what we can't see. God knows what we don't know. And God *did* answer your prayer ... because "no" *is* an answer. God just didn't answer your prayer the way *you* wanted Him to. He answered your prayer the way *He* wanted to.

> *"God is His own interpreter,*
> *and He will make it plain"*
> _____
> (WILLIAM COWPER).

Your Mother was going to die one day anyway. God just chose the time of her death. Perhaps He knows that it will take your broken heart over your Mother's death to bring you to the God Who *Loves you*. If your Mother knew the Lord Jesus as her Saviour, she's now with Him in Heaven. A Christian's death is their final "victory" over satan. You're going to die one day too, you know. Will you be going to be with your Mother ... and *your* Lord? You can, you know.

My Friend, the God Who created you *Loves you* infinitely more than you love your Mother. I *know* He does, and He wants you to be *His* Child. Then, you will *know* His Love and have "Victory in Jesus" – *and Victory* over death!

> *"When you're a Christian, your Christian loved-ones*
> *who have died are a much greater part*
> *of your future than they were of your past"*
> _____
> (GREG LAURIE).

God cannot lie, and He promises that He is working *all* things together for good (Eternal Good!) to those who love

Him (Romans 8:28). You are not one who loves God yet, but He's working on changing that by changing your heart. The Lord is washing your eyes with tears so that you can finally "see" Him.

When I witness to a hardened atheist who is in no way receptive to the Gospel of Jesus Christ, I will sometimes end with these words, "Even though you are saying that you don't believe in God, would you do this ole lady a favor and find out for sure before you die? Even though you don't pray to God, just as a favor to me, do it anyway. Pray and ask God if He really does exist. And if He does, is Jesus Christ really His Son? *And* ask Him if He sent Jesus to die for our sins on the Cross. Then, ask Him if Jesus really died for *you* – to pay the penalty for all *your* sins. Now, if God is Who He says He is, don't you think He's powerful enough to let you know He exists ... *and* that Jesus *is* His Son Who died for *you*?"

Listen with your heart, my Friend, as I say those same words to *you*. Pray to the God Who Loves you. *Don't* give up on the Lord ... because He will *never* give up on *you*!

Now, I know what you're wondering, "If there really is a God, then He already knows everything. So, why does He want us to pray?"

Answer: God just *Loves* fellowshipping with us!

I know, I know ... there are lots of other reasons too, but I'm more than a little partial to that one. And God is *really* looking forward to fellowshipping with you *for the very first time*! You could make God happy *today*.

Now, I know what you're thinking, "If God really exists, He's already happy."

Yep, and when you share your heart with Him, He makes *you* happy too. Try it.

I could be wrong about you. You're not an atheist, y*ou're* just a guy who's bored with life ... and you don't know why. Well, I'll tell you why. The reason you are so bored is because you have in-grown eyeballs. They are only looking at you ... and *you* are a boring person. You think that *you* are the center of the known Universe. No wonder you're bored. The man all wrapped up in himself makes a very small (and boring) package. The more you look only at yourself, the more you are totally consumed with self pity – always wanting to be what you aren't and to have what you don't.

Now, I know what you're thinking, "Well, if it wasn't for self-pity, I wouldn't get any sympathy at all."

Not so. *I* feel very sorry for you because a totally self-absorbed life is a totally boring life. That's the reason you do so much dumb, immoral, idiotic stuff. Your life is so boring that you *must* do those things just to exist. Therefore, "havin' fun" has become an addictive drug for you.

Satan is also having fun – with *you*. You're the devil's late-night comedy show. He's fooling you into laughing yourself all the way into hell. But good news! Jesus can fix all that ... because Jesus can fix *you*.

King Jesus is the Center of His Universe, and *He* isn't boring! You can't be bored belonging to Jesus ... no matter how hard you try. I dare you to try it. I dare you to chance looking at *Jesus* for a change. Just take a moment and look over at God's Son hanging on the Cross – bleeding and dying for *you*. *Your* sins nailed Jesus to that Cross. *Your* hard heart was the hammer that drove those nails. *Your* rebellion was the whip that beat Jesus' back. Jesus is taking *your* place there, you know. Now that's not boring to a lost sinner who desperately needs a Saviour!

Until you realize how much your sins hurt God, you will never seek His forgiveness. Until you "see" how much it cost God to Save your Eternal soul by letting His Precious Son die, you will never feel your heart break. God's Heart broke that day He had to watch His Son die hanging on a Cross. But He kept thinking of you ... and how much *He Loves precious you*.

Listen, my Friend, the Lord sent me here today to tell you that the reason Jesus is on that Cross is because He knows that you need Him to be there ... for *you*. Your soul is locked up in your flesh, and your flesh and your soul are both locked up in satan's chains!

YOU NEED JESUS!!

Come to the Lord Jesus through His Blood that He shed for you on the Cross. Just let Jesus apply His Precious Blood to your inner spirit-man, and it will break satan's chains and set you free! He whom The Son sets free is free indeed. You will even be free of your boring life ... at last.

"Some people die at 25 –
and aren't buried until they're 75"

(BENJAMIN FRANKLIN).

God is giving you the chance to die to yourself *now* and let Jesus Save you, so that you can *gloriously live* the rest of your life for *Him*. All Praise to The King of kings!

Maybe you've already had a close call with death. You almost died! But "somehow" you were *miraculously* delivered. That was *God.* He was saving you then, and now God is reaching out to "Save" you once again – this time from hell! But sadly, you don't believe that. You're the guy who thinks you're too "good" to go to hell when you die.

You're saying, "If I had been in The Garden, *I* would *never* have done what that weak Adam did. No siree, not me."

Yeah, right. Newsflash! You do it every day.

Adam handed your God-given Birthright over to satan, and now, *you* hand yourself over to him every day of your life. When you put drugs, alcohol, nicotine, pornography, etc. into your body, you have just handed yourself over to the devil. When you lie, fight, steal, engage in immoral sex, etc., you are *selling your soul to the devil. And* you're selling-out to the devil. You think that "all those wicked people" put Jesus on that Cross. *But God* is looking straight at *you* and saying, "Thou art the man!"

> *"Pride goeth before destruction,*
> *and an haughty spirit before a fall"*

(PROVERBS 16:18).

So, let me ask you this: If you can make it to Heaven by being "good," then why did God cruelly crucify His Dear Son, Jesus, on Calvary's Cross?

> *"If righteousness come by the law,*
> *then Christ is dead in vain"*

(GALATIANS 2:21).

Since you are so righteous (self-righteous), Jesus says He didn't come for you ... because He came to *Save sinners*. So, I guess you don't need Jesus to do *anything* for *you*.

Ah, but you *do*! You need Jesus for the next breath you take and the next beat of your heart. You need Jesus to take your sin and give you His *Life*! Why not start reading the Words of Jesus in the Bible until you feel the weight of your sin in the

Light of His Righteousness.

Alexander Pope describes Jesus' Miracle of turning the water into wine like this, "The conscious water saw its Master ... and blushed." God's Word is a Mirror in which you see yourself for who you really are, and you see Jesus for Who *He* really is – The Son of God! I don't remember who said it, but it's very true: "If you trust yourself ... you don't know yourself."

I know satan, and that devil's hatred for Jesus is so intense that he doesn't want *anyone* seeing Jesus *or* following Him. Therefore, satan keeps *his* followers waging war against Jesus. For instance, at Christmas, satan can't stand our celebration of the Birth of Jesus, our Saviour. So, his followers fight hard to destroy Christmas because of The One we celebrate.

Instead of getting their own holiday, they hi-jack Christmas by not allowing Jesus to attend His own Birthday Party, for pity's sake! I heard on the news about a little girl who drew a lovely picture of the Nativity for her Class Christmas Play – *but* the school banned her picture because it showed *Jesus*. *Mercy Me!*

I feel so sorry for satan's crowd, because they just don't know about the *first* Christmas tree. It had a Gift on it, and it had a Light on it. Yep, our Christmas celebration today is only possible because The Light of the World, Jesus, was willing to hang on a wooden Cross and die an horrific death in order to give Himself to us as our Saviour. In the ole days, people celebrated Christmas because they *knew* the Saviour Whose Birth they were celebrating. If you have never received God's Gift of His Son, Jesus, you have nothing to celebrate at Christmas. You can't say, "Thank You, Jesus, for coming and dying for *me!*"

Sadly, you're just a part of this lost, dark world. *But* you *could* do what the wise men did and seek Jesus. The wisest thing you could ever do is follow after the leading of The Light of the World and travel in your heart to Jesus. You'll find Him dying on a Cross – for *you*! Once there, humble yourself, knell down before His Glory and worship the Son Who was given to be the Saviour of the world ... and *you*!

The Angels are praising Jesus, the King of all Creation! When you join them in "Praise to Jesus," you will never be the same again. You will see Jesus, the Bright and Morning Star, and you will rejoice with exceeding great *joy*! The Joy of Jesus.

Many people today are like the inn-keeper – they have no room for Jesus in their heart. But *they* are the ones who are on the outside looking in. Therefore, they don't know the truth: satan loses ... big time. Jesus Wins ... Big Time! When I see how angry and sad they are following loser satan and how joyful and peaceful we Christians are following our King Jesus, I wish I could give them what we have. And *this* is my chance to do so. Big Time! We serve a Mighty God Who cannot fail!

Every one of you reading this has been given a gift – the gift of life. God, and God alone, gave you this gift. Now, He's watching you very closely to see what you're doing with this precious gift He has given you. What you do with your God-given life is your "gift" to God.

Don't grieve God by giving the gift He has given you to His enemy, satan. No, gladden God's Heart by giving Him *your* heart. Receive the Gift He has given you on the Cross (Jesus), and He will give *you* Eternal Life! Then, you'll have *three* gifts from God: Your life, Jesus, *and* Eternal Life. What a wonderful way to have a *Joyous Day* everyday!

May I ask you a very personal question? Have you ever had "the thought" to kill yourself?

Suicide is a major cause of death among our young folks, so there's a good chance you have. Need I tell you who it is giving you those thoughts? Not the God Who created you, *Loves* you and has some very important *Eternal Work* for you to do for Him.

Nope, the one who is trying to "take you out" hates you so much that he can't even see straight. *So* ... he gets you involved in drugs, alcohol, pornography, promiscuity, crime, cults, etc. to the point that *you* can't even *think* straight! Every sin you commit is a vehicle for a demon to ride on into your soul. Really! Now, you have a whole legion of demons reigning inside of you, and it's very easy for "the enemy" to put his thoughts into your mind.

I don't have a TV, so I don't watch it. But I hear tell there's a show on it that gives thirteen reasons why people commit suicide. Well, I've got news for those TV producers: Fiend satan has a whole lot more than thirteen reasons to whisper (and scream) into folks' ears as to why they should kill themselves. And he uses movies, books, web sites, games, and TV shows (like theirs) to do so.

When I was coming along, it wasn't like this. In the ole days, suicide was actually fairly rare. But today, as satan takes over the soul of our Nation, he is able to control the way people think *and* act. Have you ever noticed the connection between the people who take satan's drugs and the people who take their God-given lives? Yep, drug-invited demons scream at you, "Do it! It's the easy way out!"

No one can keep you so discombobulated as the author of sin, hate, strife, and confusion. Satan's agenda is to "take you out" by either putting you in prison or putting you in your grave. And he does it through *mind control*. But while the devil is busy screaming his lies into your ear, God's Spirit is now whispering His Truth straight to your heart. *Mercy Me!*

Satan, your worst enemy, has plenty of demonic reasons for you to kill yourself ... naturally. *But God,* your Forever Friend, has plenty of His own Divine reasons for you to live – He *created you* for Himself! I'm praying that through this book, I can "be Jesus" to you and put *God's* thoughts into your mind.

God knows that you want to die to escape all the pain you're living in. And yet, you're more than likely not in any *physical* pain. Your *soul* is in pain because of the things people have done to you and said to you. They treated you wrongly, and your mind and heart *cannot* forget or forgive. It was just too terrible.

Your soul exists in the invisible "Spiritual World." And I have news for you: No one in this physical world can truly heal your soul which lives in "Another World." Only Someone Who lives in the same World that your soul lives in can heal you. Your only Hope is Jesus Christ – the Saviour of your soul. The cure for your pain is *His* pain – the pain He suffered on the Cross ... for *you*, my Friend.

However, satan also lives in the invisible realm, and when your soul is in *his* clutches, he is your only help. Let me assure you that the devil is only interested in helping you kill yourself. He screams at you that it's the only way to cure your pain (more slave psychology).

Maybe you're living with the pain of the horrible things *you* have said and done to others. Either way, when you belong to the Lord, His great Love for you soothes over all the stinging pain of the wounds inflicted on you by evil, hurtful people ... *or* the pain of the wounds you have inflicted on others. (I know of which I speak.) So, open your heart and receive the Lord's Love and forgiveness, and don't let satan trick you into taking the coward's way out.

Maybe you're the desperate person who has a deep longing in your soul ... but you don't know what you're longing for. You've tried college, career, popularity, sex, money, marriage, drugs, travel, mystical religions, crime – you've tried it *all,* and you're still as empty and depressed as when you started out. No, even more so. You sense that "something" is missing in your life, but you just don't know what. Life is so ... pointless. You fell so ... hopeless.

Well, I'll tell you what's missing. Love is what's missing – *Jesus' Love*! Jesus' Love for you – and your love for Him – is the missing piece in the puzzle of your life. Really! In fact, I've given it some thought, and I have decided that *this* is exactly what's wrong with our messed-up Country today. A large part of our population belongs to satan, not God. Therefore, *the devil* controls their souls ... which explains why we see so many people full of anger, rage, and hate. Love and reverence for God have died; therefore, love and respect for one another have also died – especially among our young folks.

The era of "ladies and gentlemen" is a relic of days gone "bye" – and it's sad. In *modern* America, our young folks are taught that they are just evolved-animals. So, what do you expect? Purity and Godly morals are laughed at today. Pornography, lust, and immoral sex have replaced True Love for God and each other.

Satan is writing the script for the soap-opera-lives people are living these days. He tells them that love isn't true – it's just something you do. And that's why you've found that you can't trust *anyone's* love for you. *But* you still can't help longing for a love that will *never* let you down and *never* let you go.

Newsflash! You aren't longing for love – you're longing for "Someone." You have a deep craving and desire in your soul for a relationship with *God*! I know you do, because you're just like me. You are no Homecoming Queen, but when you were in grade school, you had a serious crush on "Mr. Homecoming King" … who didn't even know you existed. But it didn't matter, because you would still lie awake at night on your bed dreaming of the day he would "come to his senses" and *see* all your subtle, feminine charms and your exquisite inner beauty. Then, he would finally realize that *you* were "the one" for him, and *he* was "the one" for you … but it never happened.

Well take heart, Dear Heart, that dream has finally come true. Jesus Christ is "The Homecoming King" of the Universe, and He is infinitely better looking than your grade school heart-throb. And get this: He is infinitely in Love with *you* … right now!

The Lord Jesus sent me to tell you that Love is something *He* does too … and this is how: He leaves Heaven and comes to our Earth knowing He is here to die on a Cross … for *you*! Jesus Loves you like no one else on this Earth ever has, ever will … ever could. The Lord Jesus is the One Who floods more Love, Joy, and Peace into your heart than you ever thought possible. After which, your circumstances may not change … but *you* sure will.

However, when satan manages to separate man from his God … satan wins! Yep, when you reject the Creator God, what do you have left that you can hold onto … and can hold onto you? I'll tell you what you have left – a slippery, slimy "serpent god" who coils around you and chokes you to death. *Mercy Me!*

> *"When you lose God, you lose yourself"*
>
> (RAY STEDMAN).

Living merely a physical life in this world is so depressing that without *Jesus'* Love for you *through it all,* you will have no reason to keep on living *through it all* any longer. Jesus' Supernatural, soul-filling, heart-satisfying *Spiritual Love* (not physical people or material things) is the most important thing in life! When it is missing in your heart, you will listen to the one controlling your soul – satan, the god of hate and death. Come to Jesus and let *Him* give you His Love, His Life, and His freedom from sin and death. For a multitude of sins there is a multitude of His tender Mercies.

"For the law of the Spirit of Life in Christ Jesus hath made me free from the law of sin and death"

(ROMANS 8:2).

The Spirit of *Love* in Christ Jesus draws you to His Cross ... through which you enter into Jesus' World of *Eternal Life*!

Your life – made up of hours, days, and years – is *so precious* to God. And He wants it to be precious to *you*. Don't let the devil fool you into wasting it on satanic music, movies, parties, and drugs. No! Lift your eyes from the garbage of this Earth to your Precious Creator God. *He* won't waste your life.

Now, I know what you're thinking, "But drugs make me feel *so good*!"

Yep, instant Heaven ... *forever hell*!

Why not shock everyone around you (including satan) by spending a month listening to only great Classical Music. Really! The results will even shock *you*. Ole slewfoot will run like crazy! He absolutely *hates* music written "Soli Deo Gloria." But don't worry, the God Who created you and Loves you will still be there with you. And no doubt about it, *that's* the Truth.

When you let the Lord *Love* you and *Save* you, He not only gives you "New Life," He gives you *a Reason to live*. He gives you the Best Reason in the whole Universe – Himself! Jesus is the Helper of the helpless. He gives Hope to the hopeless. Jesus says to you, "Come unto Me ... like a little child. I will Save you and give you *My Way* out. **I AM** "The Way" out!

I AM the Way-Maker. You can trust *My Love* for you."

*"For I know the thoughts that I think toward you,
saith The Lord, thoughts of peace, and not of evil,
to give you a future and a hope"*

(JEREMIAH 29:11).

My guess is that no one has ever told you before that the Lord Jesus has a very special place for you in His Heart *and* a very important position for you in His World — as His Ambassador! Because if you only knew all the thoughts *He* is thinking about you, *you* would get a whole lot more excited about your life yourself.

Here is something else to seriously consider. Even though you may not be a Born-Again Christian yet, you still belong to God ... because you aren't the One Who *miraculously created* your spirit, soul, and body — *God* did! Your life is a "Glorious Gift" from God to you. Therefore, when you die, you *will* stand before Him accountable to Him for the life He gave you to live on this Earth. To kill yourself would make you accountable to the God Who created you for the murder of *you*! Not a good place to be. You see, killing yourself doesn't end the pain — it only makes it *eternally* worse.

Our Great God is Infinitely Wise. Therefore, He had a very good reason for creating you. Take inventory of your life. I'm sure you will find *someone* who loves you and wants you here as much as God does. Suicide is the most selfish act a person can do. You will cause *someone* much greater pain than what you are presently going through. Trust me, I have seen it too many times over my lifetime.

As I grow older, I realize that it is much easier to die than to live. You must *fight* to live! And you *will* fight to live ... when you have hope. Rejoice! You have *Hope*! His Name is Jesus Christ. He is the Eternal King, the Lord of Glory, and the God of all comfort.

So, listen to *God's* Voice. *He will get you through this.* If God were finished with you on this Earth, He wouldn't need *your* help to get you into Heaven. Nope, the only one you're thinking about helping here is the enemy of God – satan himself. *Mercy Me!*

Your "Eternal Soul" is of more value to the God of this Universe than you could ever imagine! He created you uniquely for Himself, and He is just waiting for you to give yourself to Him. When you do, He takes you, touches you deep in your spirit, washes your sins away with Jesus' Precious Blood, heals you, makes you whole and makes you *His*. Then, He totally transforms you and uses you *mightily*! You can't begin to imagine all that God will do with you ... when you are *His*. Are you ready?

Maybe you're like the folks I witness to who say, "If God would just show me a Miracle, I would believe in Him."

Right. Well, I will tell *you* what I tell them. Go look in the mirror, for pity's sake. *You* are "a walking Miracle!" How do you think miraculously-designed-and-*supernaturally*-created-you got here? Oh, I forgot ... *you* evolved from a single-celled bacterium in a primordial swamp, right? Well, at least that explains a few things. *But God created me!* And He created you too – "Fearfully and Wonderfully!"

When the Light of Christ dawns on you, enabling you to finally "see" that you were *created* by a Powerful, Super Intelligent, Supernatural Being – God, it will totally transform your dark soul. *You,* my Friend, are undeniably convincing *proof* of God on this Earth, because you were created by Him in the "Imago Dei!"

Look out into our enormous Universe. It works in perfect precision and unison — the same Supernatural, Super Intelligent way your own body works within *you*. Scientifically *proven*! When you see a Creation, you know there *has to be* a Creator. Your house didn't "just create" itself, and neither did our Universe, your body … *or* your *soul*! I *know* the Creator. His Name is the Lord Jesus Christ. And you can *know* Him too! Then, the swamp creatures will no longer be your ancestors. Hallelujah!

Last, but not least, look into your own heart. God has placed Eternity in your heart as surely as He has placed precision in the Universe and in your own miraculous body.

> *"Do you sense an other-world ache and yearning*
> *when you sit in a funeral service or stand beside the casket …*
> *or graveside … of a friend or loved one? Why is that?*
> *Where does that longing come from?*
> *It did not slither from the slime!*
> *It did not climb up the ladder of evolutionism*
> *by the law of tooth and claw!*
> *It came from the Heart of Almighty God*
> *Who Created you for Himself and is your Father,*
> *calling you Home by His Spirit"*
>
> (RICK DEIGHTON,
> MORE THAN CONQUERORS
> IN CULTURAL CLASHES).

You can't escape hoping beyond hope that there is more to your life than just these few pitiful years you're living right now. In your heart of hearts, you're praying there really *is* "Another World" to go to when your present body eventually dies. *And* you're hoping that "Someone" is there to Love you more than you have ever been loved before. *God* is The One Who is speaking to you deep in your heart, and *that* is a Miracle too! *Now* is the time you finally listened to Him.

"I go to prepare a Place for you …
that where **I AM,** *there ye may be also."*
Signed: Jesus

(JOHN 14:2).

Now, you may be the guy who says, "I can't believe in a God Who allows so much bad stuff to happen in the world." *(Hmmm).*

Your problem is that you don't *know* this God you're judging. I know Him, and I know that God doesn't need me to defend Him. God defends Himself … in His Word. Just open a Bible, and there you'll find your "Answers in Genesis." Because of Adam and Eve's sin, we are *all* living in a sin-cursed world … as you can see. They handed all of mankind's God-given Birthright (along with themselves and all of us) and the Title Deed to Planet Earth over to satan. *Mercy Me!*

So, don't blame God for all the "bad stuff" *satan* is doing. Our All-Wise God is letting you see what the world looks like when satan runs it. Just be "thankful" that things are as good as they are, instead of complaining that things are "so bad."

"We can complain because rose bushes have thorns,
or rejoice because thorn bushes have roses"

(ABRAHAM LINCOLN).

The question isn't: Why do bad things happen to good people? (because there aren't any), but: Why do good things ever happen to us bad people? Only God's Grace allows *any* good to still exist in our sin-cursed world. Of course, God's Greatest Grace was sending His Son, Jesus, to our fallen world to redeem us from the curse. The Love of Jesus is the Greatest Good in the midst of all the evil that exists. In love, He's *allowing* that "bad stuff" to happen to you for the purpose of driving you to the only Good Thing in this Universe – Himself!

So, don't expect Almighty God to give puny you all His answers here on this Earth. Just know that He isn't biting His fingernails over all the bad stuff satan is doing – because the devil truly is *God's* devil. You don't have to blow a fuse trying to figure God out. Just rest assured that *God* has it all figured out.

> *"The Lord hath prepared His Throne in Heaven,*
> *and His Kingdom ruleth over all!"*

(PSALM 103:19).

Bless the Lord, O my soul!

You're saying that you can't believe in God because He allows "bad stuff" to happen. But how can you even know what is "bad" and what is "good" without God? The only way for you to know "good" from "evil" is for there to be a "moral law" within your soul. *So* ... where does that moral law come from?

You say, "From me. I'm my own god, remember?"

(Hmmm).

Well, if you don't believe in God, you believe in evolution. Therefore, you evolved from the animals, and animals have no moral law. So, you still haven't explained to me where *your* moral law comes from. And trust me, you break those moral laws every day of your life because you belong to "the original moral-law-breaker," satan himself. *Mercy Me!*

I never have to wonder why "bad" things happen to *me*. I belong to the Lord Jesus. I love Him with all my heart, and I walk with Him every day. I'm not perfect, but I *am* "perfectly forgiven!" And today, I spend my life telling other folks how *they* can be forgiven of *their* sins and belong to the Lord too.

Satan hates that, and he hates *me.* He would kill me ... if he could. The devil's only mantra in his evil "weirderland" concerning *me* is, "Off with her head!"

In the book of Job in the Bible, we see what satan loves to do to folks who love the Lord. But that doesn't worry me, because I know that the trouble the devil throws at me to take me down, my Lord will use to take me up higher – and *that* makes satan even madder (hee-hee). Oh well, that's what happens to those who rebel against the Lord – they always end up *the loser.*

> *"Be of good cheer, it is I; be not afraid."*
> *Signed: Jesus*
>
> ———————
> (MARK 6:50).

Take the looooong look into Eternity, my Friend. Are you sure you want to remain in the clutches of *the loser* in "The Epic Battle of the Universe" for the souls of men? Selah.

The Apostle John wrote the Book of The Revelation to reveal the Lord Jesus Christ. This daring book is my revelation of satan. It unveils and reveals him for who he is, what he is and what he does.

Rush Limbaugh says of the ungodly, "We know these people don't wear underwear because when you undress them (spiritually speaking) ... they're naked."

Ditto for satan. He seems so well-dressed and respectable ... *until* you expose him for what he actually is – a dirty demon in disguise. Satan knows how to dress for success so that he can fool you into following him into dismal failure. That shifty devil is the "talking snake" behind all the evil in our world. The master liar deceives you by promising, "Do 'this', and it will satisfy all your deepest longings." So, you believe his lie, do "it" and find yourself even deeper in your pit of despair. *Mercy Me!*

Multitudes of people all over this world are enslaved by that seductive demon ... and they don't even realize it! At least now, *you* can never again say that you don't know for sure who *you* belong to. And you can never again say that you don't know for sure that Jesus *is* Merciful and Jesus *will* Save. He came, He died, He arose, and He Lives today to give *you* Eternal Life. Praise His Holy Name!

Maybe you're the guy who has been abused and lied to all your life, and you figure I'm just one more. So, how do you know if *I'm* telling you the Truth? You don't. You don't find the Truth by looking to a person. You find the Truth by going deep into your own soul through *prayer* and miraculously discovering the Spirit of Jesus *there* ... speaking to your heart. Then, you ask Jesus if *He* is telling you the Truth. "The Truth" is actually the Person of the Spirit of Christ Who speaks to you in your soul ... deeper than anyone else has ever gone before!

Go to a *Bible*-believing, *Bible*-preaching, *Christ*-centered, *Jesus*-loving, *Jesus*-lifting-up Church and listen for *God* to speak to you through His Servant. *Read the Bible!* Pray and listen. Listen for *Christ's* Voice speaking to your heart through His Word:

MOLLY MCCOY

*"**I AM** The Way,*
The Truth and The Life!"

(JOHN 14:6).

Make up your mind and purpose in your heart to seek the Lord *personally.* I can guarantee you: *He* is seeking *you Personally.* When Jesus speaks to you, His Voice is so sweet that the birds hush their singing. The *Melody* He sings to you is the loveliest, most compelling Song you have ever heard – or *felt.*

"This is My Beloved Son in
Whom I am well pleased, hear ye Him!"
Signed: God

(MATTHEW 17:5).

Maybe you're just afraid of what your friends will say (and think) if *you* "of all people" become a *Christian*! They're probably telling you that Christians are just a bunch of sissies. Well, Jesus was anything *but* a sissy the day He willingly died on that Cross for sinners like them (and all the rest of us).

A "real man" humbles himself and becomes a "real servant" – like Jesus did. The Lord Jesus came to Planet Earth to be a Courageous Servant. And He is *still* a Servant. Just humble *yourself* and ask Him to forgive you and "Save" you. Then, you will find out that what I'm telling you is true.

During Jesus' first earthly ministry, the Jews were wanting a Messiah who would defeat their enemy, Rome, and deliver them. *But Jesus* (the True Messiah) defeated their *real* enemy, satan, and delivered them from *him.* And He's still doing the same thing today. Jesus is our "Servant King."

Only Jesus can show you what a "real man" looks like: *A real man loves Jesus!* Your friends wouldn't know anything about *that*, and anyone who keeps you from Jesus Christ (your Divine Friend Who Loves you more than anyone else in the entire Universe!) is *not* your friend. Jesus knows that you won't make it through life very well (or end up in a good place) with *your* friends. You need the Friend Who sticketh closer than a brother.

So, don't keep "going down" with a bunch of losers – *Eternal losers*. Instead, go down to the Cross, and the Lord Jesus will lift you up!

> *"This is The Father's Will Who hath sent Me,*
> *that of all which He hath given unto Me*
> *I should lose nothing;*
> *but should raise it up again at the last day."*
> Signed: Jesus
>
> ————
> (JOHN 6:39).

These same "friends" are probably telling you that Christianity is just a crutch for weak people. But they are wrong. Christianity isn't a crutch for weak people. Christianity is a whole Hospital for dead people ... who need to be raised from the dead to "New Life in Christ!" Dr. Jesus, our well-qualified Servant King/Shepherd Saviour, is *always* on duty to empower us to live His "New Life" in *us*!

Dr. Jesus starts by *Supernaturally* performing our "Miracle Birth" – during which He gives us a Blood transfusion and a heart transplant. This allows the Spirit of our Supernatural Surgeon to actually enter into *us*! Then comes brain surgery to renew our minds by washing it with His Word. Next, nerve replacement to give us the courage to witness for Him. He even gives us a new stomach so that satan's food makes us sick! And you never have to spend hours in the waiting room before seeing Jesus. Nope, He is there when you need *a Doctor* ... not an appointment.

Your good-time-Charlie-rock-n-roll friends (who love having a high-ole-time livin' the low-life) have convinced you that we

Christians live lives that are *fatally boring.* So, steer clear of us lest you catch our deadly disease. Well, let me say that I do understand your friends because I know where they're coming from … and I also know where they're headed. Nonetheless, in my last moments of life before dying of boredom, give me equal time to describe to you my boring life.

I also have a Best Friend. My constant Companion, Jesus (Who is King of the Universe!) loves me enough to come to Planet Earth for the purpose of hanging on a wooden Cross and dying for *me*! But there's more! He has Divinely revealed Himself to me, mercifully "Saved" my Eternal soul, and now "Lives!" His Resurrected Life *in* my spirit and *through* my soul and body. Wow!

Today, and every day, we share a deep Love and an exciting Life as we talk and walk together through this world … giving His Glorious Gospel to lost folks He came to Redeem. *And* He shows Himself Faithful to me in one amazing Miracle after another!

But wait! There's even more! The most exciting part happens when my Lord frees me from this aging Earthsuit, and I fly away to spend *all* of Eternity in Heaven with my Heavenly Father, Jesus (my Saviour), the Angels, and all the Saints! A life shared with the Lord Jesus is anything *but* boring. In fact, He has even written a book through me … and *you're* in it. And *now,* He has put said book into your hands.

But wait! There's even more! The reason He has done this is to give *you* the opportunity to join all of us in Heaven for all of Eternity when the date on your Earthsuit expires. *Mercy Me!*

Maybe you're the guy who says, "I don't need Jesus. I'm a very 'spiritual' person without Him, and I go to fortune tellers who tell me what I don't know."

Well, let *me* tell you what you don't know. Those guys are all a bunch of phonies.

You say, "How can you say that about those nice people?" Because if they *really* knew the future, they would win every lottery and make billions on the stock market. And yet, they never win any lotteries or make any fortunes on Wall Street ... and that's why they have to make their money off of *you*!

"Well ... they just don't want to be corrupted by all that filthy money."

Right. And now I know why you pay them to tell you what you don't know – you'll believe *anything*!

Why don't you wise-up and come to The One Who really *does* know everything and will give you everything you need. And He won't charge you for it either. Nope, He has already paid for it *Himself*! His Name is Jesus, and I'm one of His satisfied customers. Trust me, He knew you and me long before we were ever born.

So, let *Jesus* tell you your future using my pen. As long as you belong to your slave-master/prison-warden, satan, you will have a life of never-ending trouble and ever-present pain ... because the devil is a hateful, cruel taskmaster. He steals your peace, kills your joy, and destroys your soul. He over-promises and under-delivers every time. Eventually, you will breathe your last breath, and your tortured soul will leave your cursed body to go spend all of Eternity in endless torment in the place of Eternal death. *Mercy Me!*

However, you're still trying to convince me that you don't need Jesus, "I really am a very 'spiritual' person, and I believe there are many ways to God."

Well, in the Garden of Gethsemane just before His crucifixion, Jesus was asking His Father for some way other than the Cross too. So, He fell on His face and earnestly prayed, "O My Father, *if it be possible,* let this Cup pass from Me: nevertheless, not as I will, but as Thou wilt" (Matthew 26:39).

By His loud silence that dark night, God the Father shouted to the world, "The only Way to Me is through My Son, Jesus! There is *no other way* for you to be Saved from your sins than by My Son's death on the Cross for *you*."

That is why Jesus can proclaim to you today, "**I AM** *The Way!*"

If you are trusting in any other way, you will be sorely disappointed. When you are taking your last breath, you will finally *know* that it takes a lot more than just "a way" to get you into Heaven. It takes "A Person" – Who Lives there! It takes the Holy Son of God Who *is* "The Way."

I know Him, and so can *you.* You don't need another "religion," my Friend, you need *Jesus Christ*!

"Enter ye in at the strait gate ... because strait is the gate,
and narrow is The Way which leadeth unto Life ...
and few there be who find (Him)"

(MATTHEW 7:13-14).

Perhaps you're the guy who says, "I don't think a person can know for sure they're going to Heaven when they die."

You're partially right. A person *can't* know for sure they're going to Heaven ... *unless* ... they know for sure that they *know* The One Who gives them Eternal Life in Heaven. *That's* the game-changer. And there's a verse for that:

> *"And this is the record, that God hath given to you Eternal Life, and this Life is in His Son. He that hath The Son hath Life, and he that hath not The Son hath not Life. And we know that The Son of God is come, and hath given unto us an understanding that we may know Him Who is True, and we are in Him Who is True, in His Son Jesus Christ. This is the True God and Eternal Life"*
>
> _____
>
> (I JOHN 5:11-12,20).

Amen!

The One Who miraculously *Saved* me and now *Lives* in me has a Place for me with Him in Heaven ... for sure!

You may be thinking, "How odd of God to choose to Save my Eternal soul through the death of His Son on a Cross."

Well, *I'm* thinking, "How much odder of *you* to choose to reject that Sacred Miracle of God's Gracious Gift to you ... because *if you do*, you will *still* be in satan's clutches when you breathe your last ... for sure." *Mercy Me!*

People go to hell because they choose to go to hell. But just remember, Jesus chose to go to hell too. Jesus willingly chose to suffer *your* hell on the Cross. Then, He chose to go to hell and proclaim His *Victory* over satan to the spirits there. Today, He is *still* proclaiming His Victory over satan to people on this Earth ... through us Christians.

If you feel like you're in hell today, my Friend, take heart. Jesus is with you in your hell. He's reaching out to you *right now*. If you will take His Divine Hand of Mercy, Love, and Grace with your hand of Faith, He will walk you out of your "hell." *But* you must humble yourself and *let Him.*

"Verily I say unto you, whosoever shall not receive
the Kingdom of God as a little child
shall in no wise enter therein."
Signed: Jesus
_____
(LUKE 18:17).

Receive Jesus, the Christ — the King of God's Kingdom! And when you do, to your amazement, you will discover that the only thing the fires of hell destroyed ... were the ropes that had you bound.

So, how is the Lord able to deliver you from hell? Listen with your heart, my Child, and I will tell you.

When the Lord Jesus came to this Earth, He came as "God Incarnate" (God in human flesh). When Jesus went to the Cross, He went as "God Incarnate." As God, Jesus could have slain all His enemies with a Word! He didn't *have to* die on that Cross or shed one drop of His Precious Blood. Nope. So, why did He?

I'll tell you why He did it. He knew that today — *right now* — you would need for Him to *still* be on His Eternal Cross.... as the "Sacrificial Payment" for all of *your* sins. And now, He is patiently waiting for you to come to Him and accept *His death* on your behalf. As Dallas Holm sings: He knew you then, He knows you now. He loved you then, He loves you now. And He died for *you*!

The Cross of Jesus Christ is *Eternal*! His Precious Blood is *Eternal* ... and is being spilled out for *YOU*! God's Perfect Lamb is being sacrificed on His Eternal Cross for *your* sins. In the Spiritual Realm in a *Supernatural Way*, Jesus is *still* on the Cross ... waiting for you ... just for *you*.

"Greater Love hath no man than this, that a Man lay down His Life for His friends." Signed: Jesus

(JOHN 15:13).

There is *something* about the Cross – the one that God's Son is on. That's it! It's Supernatural! Even more amazing is that you can *supernaturally* touch The One Who is on it. The first "Supernatural act" you ever do is touch the crucified Christ with a heart of *Faith* … the Faith *He* gives you (Ephesians 2:8-9).

"That means *even my Faith* is Supernatural!" (You catch on quick.)

The Lord Jesus is now offering you the Faith to believe. So, open your *spiritual eyes*, reach out with your *spiritual hand of Faith* and touch the nail-prints in His hands and the wound in His side. And when you do, the Love of Jesus that He has for you in *His* heart will enter into *your* heart. Don't be unbelieving but believing … in *Jesus*!

On the other hand, you may be doubting everything I've said so far, and you're convinced that I'm just a nut. *But* the moment you dare to do what I once did, you will join this nut on Jesus' Family Tree. You see, the genealogy of Jesus is a list of the people God used to give birth to His Son on Planet Earth. And today, *I* am someone God has used to give *Spiritual* birth to His Son on Earth!

Preachers tell us that Jesus came to Earth the first time when He was born in Bethlehem, and He will come back again at the Second Coming of Christ. But I know otherwise. The Lord Jesus came to this Earth *another* time – the day He *Saved* me and was *Born-Again* in *me*! Today, I'm *a walking Miracle*, because Jesus is "Living" His Life again in *me*! That's how *I* know Jesus came out of that tomb!

Now the Lord would *Love* to be Born-Again in *you*! And you need for Him to do just that, because your spirit was DOA when you were born, remember? That's why you feel such a "deadness" in your soul. You need Jesus Christ – the Saviour of the world – the Saviour of *your soul*!

At "The Judgment," Judge Jesus will say to the rebellious, wicked people, "Depart from Me! I never knew you!" If you want Jesus Christ to know *you*, He will recognize you when He sees His own Precious Blood stained on your spirit-man and His White Robe of Righteousness covering you as well. There's no other way.

"And when I see the Blood,
I Will *pass over you,*
and the plague shall not be upon you to destroy you!"
Signed: God

(EXODUS 12:13).

The Lord knows you need Him. Do *you* know you need Him? You do *now*! At this very moment, you are in the Holy Presence of God ... but satan doesn't want you to know it. Nor does the devil want you to know that the Lord Jesus has been waiting all your life for *this moment* – the moment that His Father would draw *you* to the foot of His Cross where He is dying to Save you. And now, He's dying to meet you.

However, ole slewfoot is frantically trying to block God's Supernatural Light from opening your "Spiritual eyes." Noooo!! The devil doesn't want you to finally "see" The Messiah and cry out from deep in your heart, "Jesus! You are dying for *me* on that Cross! You're paying for *my* sins there. Oh, thank You, Lord!"

It's true, you don't need to know for sure when Jesus died, exactly where He died, or the details of how He died. You just need to know *why* He died. And now, you do.

Satan is holding his breath and hoping that you won't realize what's happening. In all of Time and Eternity, *THIS* is your Divine Appointment – *the Time of your Visitation* from the God of this Universe! God's Irresistible Love and Awesome Power are reaching out to you *right now*. This is *your* "date with Deity."

You may be just a boy with a bus ticket and a dream ... but good news! Jesus Christ is waiting to meet your bus! And just wait until you see all the Gifts He has for you. God, and God alone, is able to create something out of nothing. Take a good look at your life. Are you ready?

If not, take my advice and take a good look at your *bus driver*. Yep, and he hasn't been taking you anywhere good ... just down one dead-end street after another. Satan loves cruising up Humanism Blvd. and down Atheism Avenue picking up more passengers just as spiritually dead as you are (right now).

Yes siree, he's gleefully driving all of you down Broadway ... heading toward Destruction Drive. Have you ever considered how much you're having to pay satan to get to keep riding on his bus? The price isn't right. It's way too high. *Eternally* too high! When Jesus stops satan's bus ... JUMP!!

However, ole slewfoot doesn't want you to wise-up and see The Light. He doesn't want you to look down the corridors of Time into Eternity and "see" that you *will* be there ... either in hell with him or in Heaven with God. And he sure doesn't want you to get the idea that decisions you make on this Earth have anything to do with your Destiny, both now and forever. You see, Eternal Life isn't just a long time or a faraway place. Eternal Life is a very real, very personal, and very intimate "Relationship" with God through his Son, the Lord Jesus (John

17:3). Yours can begin *right now*. Yes!

Satan screams, "Nooooo!!" The deceiver wants to keep you wearing his demonic dark glasses so that you can't see the Light of the World, Jesus Christ. That way, you stay stone-cold dead in your trespasses and sins ... just the way he likes you ... just the way you are.

"I AM The Light of the World; he that followeth Me shall not walk in darkness, but shall have The Light of Life!"
Signed: JESUS

(JOHN 8:12).

The devil doesn't want you to know how *precious* life is ... how Supernatural! Life is an amazing Mystery. Life is an amazing Miracle of an Awesome God Who longs for you to *really live* by coming to intimately *know* the Supreme Life of this Universe – *Himself*!

God knew that you could never have made it to Him all bogged down in your sin, and that is why He has come to *you*. *But* the adversary doesn't want you to *feel* the Divine closeness of God's Presence. Ole slewfoot doesn't want you knowing that the Lord is with you ... right here ... right now!

Nooooo!! Satan is so afraid that you might reach out with your hand of Faith and touch the Hand of God's Grace. Neverrrr!! Satan knows that all it takes is *one Touch* from God to change you, your life, and your Destiny ... *forever*! The devil knows how ready God is to breathe the Breath of Spiritual Life into *you* just as He did into His first man, Adam. God is just waiting for the Word from you – the Word of Faith....which God gives you when you humble yourself and ask.

Since satan knows that God has the Power to "Save" you and deliver you out of his clutches, he's getting very nervous right now. So, ole slewfoot is quickly pulling out every trick in his playbook to keep you in *his* power. He doesn't want you to know how badly you need God — how badly you need the Supernatural, Spiritual Life *only God* can give you.

Your demonic slave-master is hoping you don't know how close God is to you right now. That ole devil is so afraid he's about to lose you as his slave. So, he starts screaming, "Don't listen!!" as Jesus knocks on your heart's door, and Christ's Spirit whispers in your spiritual ear, "If you will dare to open your heart's door to Me, *I will come in*! I really will. My Spirit will *Supernaturally* dwell in your spirit (your inner-man) and you won't be spiritually dead anymore!"

> *"Seek ye The Lord while He may be found.*
> *Call upon Him while He is near!"*
>
> ---
> (ISAIAH 55:6).

Satan wants you believing that the Spiritual World is a quadrillion miles away. But it isn't. Nope, we're living in this physical world within the Spiritual World ... *or* we're living in the Spiritual World within this physical world. Don't think about it too long, or you'll blow a mental fuse. What I'm saying is, "Jesus is a whole lot closer to you than you think He is." *Mercy Me!*

My Friend, you will never "Pray!" as you should, "Praise!" as you should, "Love!" as you should, or "Live!" as you should until you Supernaturally "See!" that you are in *the very Presence of the Lord* every moment of your life! Thank Him ... *right now*!

However, ole slewfoot never gives up, and he has another devilish plan to keep you from ever meeting your Saviour. He tells you, "You can believe in Jesus ... but only as a mere man, a good moral teacher, or an important person in history."

Yeah ... the devil doesn't care if you believe *that*. In fact, that's what he wants you to believe. He just doesn't want you to know the Truth: Jesus is *God,* and He has the Supernatural Power to Save your Eternal soul and give you Eternal Life ... and that Power is in His Blood (the Life is in the Blood). Satan is scared to death of the Blood of Jesus Christ!

Much to satan's great dismay, when you say "YES!" to Jesus, His Spiritual Blood will flow over your soul and wash you clean of every sin you have ever committed. The devil is terrified that you'll experience the Power of Jesus' *Sacrificial Death* on your behalf ... which "Saves" you from all your sin for all Eternity! God's Blood flowing out of Jesus' body on the Cross is paying the tremendous debt you owe God for all those sins you've committed. The Lord Jesus Saves from the gutter-most to the utter-most. Hallelujah! Thank You, Lord Jesus.

> *"Jesus didn't come to just inform us.*
> *Jesus came to totally Transform us!"*
>
> (ALISTAIR BEGG).

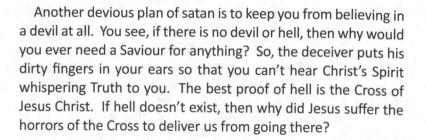

Another devious plan of satan is to keep you from believing in a devil at all. You see, if there is no devil or hell, then why would you ever need a Saviour for anything? So, the deceiver puts his dirty fingers in your ears so that you can't hear Christ's Spirit whispering Truth to you. The best proof of hell is the Cross of Jesus Christ. If hell doesn't exist, then why did Jesus suffer the horrors of the Cross to deliver us from going there?

Satan hopes you didn't hear that. He loves keeping you blinded to the existence of the very real demonic realm ... where he is ... clutching *you* in his grimy hand. *Mercy Me!*

I was witnessing to an atheist one time and said to him, "Satan has you blinded." When he heard that, he started laughing so hard I considered sending him a bill for the medicine he was receiving from all the good laughter he was experiencing.

When he could talk, he said, "Satan?! Don't tell me you believe in such mythical characters as *satan*! Ha! Ha! Ha!"

Hell is a very real place of *very real* pain and everlasting torment ... waiting for those who reject the Saviour, Jesus Christ. How do I know? Jesus Himself spoke of hell more than anyone else in the Bible, because *He created hell* for spiritual rebels who don't want to spend Eternity in Heaven – like satan. And satan delights in keeping *you* a spiritual rebel too.

Therefore, the devil tells you how smart, sophisticated and good you are. So, you certainly don't need Jesus to die on a Cross for *you*. Nope, not you. Ole slewfoot wants you listening to *him* – not God's Holy Spirit Who is speaking to you right now. Oh no, satan likes having you for his slave too much. So, he sure doesn't want you to receive God's Truth, humble yourself and come to the foot of the Cross where Jesus is dying for you ... because satan knows that when you look up into the eyes of Jesus, you will see, for the first time in your life, His great **Love** for *YOU*!

That's the devil's worst nightmare. He wants you to keep a rebellious, hard heart – like his. *But Jesus* wants to break your heart, then take your heart and give you a soft heart of Love – like His. Be brave. Hand Jesus the hammer and *let Him*!

*"Jesus is in the business of breaking
proud hearts and healing wounded hearts"*

(JONI ERICKSON TADA).

Jesus can't come into a proud, hard heart. He can only enter in through the cracks of a humble, broken heart. Your sins break Jesus' Heart. Now it's time they broke yours. The things I've been saying to you aren't meant to hurt you. They are meant to break you ... because you need to be broken. And only God can truly break you.

"My job as your Pastor is to beat you up with Jesus!"
                                 (TONY EVANS).

Now, I know what you're thinking, "It's not nice to beat people up."

Newsflash! You're *already* beat-up ... by satan! *But Jesus* is wanting to "whip you into shape" as a loving Father. Satan is wanting to "beat you into submission" as a cruel slave-driver. Which do *you* want?

"The Lord must bring you down
before He can lift you up"
                               (ALISTAIR BEGG).

As the Lord drives a stake through your heart, why don't *you* drive a stake into Eternity and say, *"This* is *the day* I lay it all down before You, Lord Jesus, and let Your Precious Blood wash all my vile sins away. You bid me come to You ... just as I am. So, I'm coming, Lord, without one argument or excuse. I'm letting Your Blood that You shed for me on the Cross be for sin a double cure. It "Saves" me from God's wrath and makes me *pure* in His sight. O, Jesus, Lamb of God ... I come to Thee! Amen."

However, "you know who" doesn't want you to experience the sweet Peace of God that comes to you when all your sins have been wiped away by the Precious Blood of Jesus, God's Son. The devil doesn't want you to have the calm assurance of knowing that you are a Redeemed Child of God with a Home in Heaven when you die.

OLE SLEWFOOT

"Therefore, being justified by Faith,
we have Peace with God through our Lord Jesus Christ"

(ROMANS 5:1).

Ole slewfoot doesn't want you to know that you are firmly in the death-throes of his grip. Nope, he wants you to stay just the way you are right now – dead in your trespasses and sins.

So, the question before the House once again is: What do *you* want? I know what God wants. I know what the Christians praying for you want. I know what I want. In fact, I am praying for everyone who reads this book. I'm asking God's Holy Spirit to quicken the words of this book to the heart of the reader and "Supernaturally Save" every lost soul who reads it!

Big Prayer. **Bigger GOD!!**

The Lord Jesus was "The Master Story-Teller." He once told the story of a guy who ran to his neighbor's home at midnight to beg for some food to give a visiting friend because his own cupboard was bare. That's the story of you (and me) ... and God. We have nothing to give anyone ... until God first gives *us* what *we* need.

Right now, you need to know that *you need God* to give you what you need ... because it's as black as midnight in your life. Like the man in the story, you need to run to the Light of the World, Jesus, for His Love and Forgiveness ... because your soul is so bare. Just come to the Lord and "ASK" (ask, seek, knock). Confess your sin to Him, ask His forgiveness and receive His death for you. Then, He will give you His Holy Spirit – *forever*! (Luke 11:5-13). O, the deep, deep Love of Jesus.

The Lord Jesus met *my* Eternal need at the foot of His Cross years ago. That's when I learned that the most important factors for having a great life on Earth and a *Fantastic Forever* are … location, location, location.

Now, I'm not talking here about where you live geographically. Oh no, you can have an empty, miserable life living in a Palacios mansion by the ocean, *or* you can have an abundantly full, gloriously satisfying life living in a small van. The bottom-line question is, "Who fills your life?"

When your life is lived "in Christ," then Jesus Christ (the Fullness of God) is also living "in you." "Christ in you" brings the Fullness and Glory of His Divine Life to *your very soul*! Now you're under the Spout where the Glory comes out. *But* … when your life is lived "in the world" (apart from Christ) can you guess who fills you *then*? Yep, ole slewfoot. And the more he fills you up, the emptier you get. The more of his "demonic life" he pours in, the deader you become. Now you're under the gun where the death comes out. Is that you?

> Are you slowly derailing? Are you just one more bad decision away from a train wreck?
>
> Does satan have you wired so tight that you're just one more string-snap away from a major meltdown?
>
> Is your life one big blowout?
>
> Is your soul mortgaged to the devil?
>
> Is "the note" due, and you're flat broke?
>
> Well, my Friend, I know Someone Who will pay it for you … but you have to *come* to Him and "let Him."

OLE SLEWFOOT

When Adam and Eve sinned, there was hell to pay. Actually, there was a Holy God to pay. And God the Son came Himself to pay the debt *Himself* that we all owe God. Amazing! It's called the Amazing Grace of God through Jesus, His Son ... extended to *you*! Only the sacrificial death of the innocent, sinless Lamb of God could satisfy the wrath of the Heavenly Father Who had been betrayed by sinful man.

Are you ready to wake up from your satan-induced coma, look around and figure out whose world you're living in? When you finally wise-up and decide that you would rather live your life "in Christ" – in Jesus' World – you will find "The Key" that unlocks the Door at the foot of His Eternal Cross. It's called "The Precious Blood of Jesus Christ." You *must* let it wash your soul clean of every sin. And *then*, you can come on in. We're all waiting here with Jesus ... for *you*!

As Jesus' "New Creation" you can go from being satan's victim to being the Lord's Victor ... in a heartbeat! Wouldn't you rather be "in Christ," living "in Jesus' World," so that you can one day go live "in Heaven" ... *forever*!?

Location! Location! Location!

My early life was spent in a satan-induced comma – living as one of his slaves. *But*, "Praise the Lord," *He* is allowing me to end my life a whole lot better than I started out ... and He will do the same for you. Just give your life (and yourself) over to Him and watch what He does with it. Get ready to be "Blessed!"

"The Father loveth The Son, and hath
given all things into His hand"

(JOHN 3:35).

A Sunday School teacher asked her class, "Children, what do you have to do to be forgiven of your sin?" A little boy blurted out, "You have to sin!" So, praise God, *you* qualify to be forgiven of your sin … all of it.

The same teacher asked her class, "Children, what do you have to do to go to Heaven?"

The same little boy blurted out, "You have to die!"

God's Holy Spirit has convicted you of your sin (which probably wasn't very hard to do☺) and has convinced you of God's Truth (casting out satan's lies). *Now* it's time you *let Him* take you out of satan's evil kingdom of darkness and seal you into the Kingdom of God's Dear Son! (Colossians 1:13). For that to happen, Jesus isn't the only one who has to die.

Salvation is a *Supernatural Miracle* of God the Father, God the Son, and God the Holy Spirit. It occurs when: (a) God reveals His Son *to* you, (b) You receive Jesus' death *for* you, (c) Christ's Spirit comes to "live" *in* you. The "in you" part is what my book *Dare to Be Jesus* is about — which doesn't apply to you … *unless* … Jesus really *is* "in you."

So, is He? Is Jesus really "in you"? Did you go to the Cross and meet Jesus there? Did you finally realize how badly you need the Saviour of this world to be *your* Saviour? He has already died for you. Did you *let* Him? Did you hear Jesus' still small Voice calling *your* name? Did you respond to Him from deep down in your inner-most being — the *real you* who is leaving your earthly body the moment it dies? Well, what are you waiting for?

Maybe you think you've been too bad for the Lord to ever want you. Not so. You can't deal God a "bad hand." The Saviour of this world *Loves* to take the worst of the worst and transform them into the Best of the best. Even if you aren't the worst of the worst, Jesus is still longing to get very personal with you and turn your life into a Cinderella Story!

The silent clock is ticking, you can feel it in your heart, and it's almost midnight in your life. You are blindly running away from the King's Son Who is pursuing you with His Love! You feel so unworthy to be His Bride. But don't. No matter your shoe size, His Divine Glass Slipper is custom-made by Him just for *you*. It will fit perfectly. Then, your Prince will miraculously deliver you from your evil stepmother (satan) and bring you, His Betrothed Bride, into His Heavenly Kingdom ... *forever*! Consider this book Jesus' Divine Invitation to His Royal Ball, aka The Marriage Supper of The Lamb. RSVP to Jesus ASAP!

> *"The Gift of God is Eternal Life*
> *through Jesus Christ our Lord!"*
>
> ---
> (ROMANS 6:23).

So, I guess we are finally going to find out what happens when The Irresistible Force meets the immoveable object. But before you make your final decision to be a rock and an island for the rest of your life, let me give you some sage advice: "You'd better let *Jesus* Love you before it's too late!"

Don't spend your life standing on the corner of the world holding a cardboard sign that reads: "Homeless." No! Come on into Jesus' World. Accept your Heavenly Bridegroom's Proposal, and you will suddenly discover that you are a Member-in-good-standing of Jesus' big Forever Family, aka The Church. You don't have to live in "spiritual Lo Debar" any longer. Nope, and you can even dine at King Jesus' Table from now on. Oh yes! There's a *Special Place* reserved just for *you*! The King is waiting to serve you Himself.

In Jesus' Big Family you will never run shy of Brothers and Sisters who love you with the Love of our Lord. Just come. You'll see. I promise. No, Jesus promises, and you can take *His* promises all the way to The Bank of Heaven. They never expire! Peter Pan isn't the only one who lives in Never Never Land. Our Lord Jesus does too.

He will *never* break a promise to you, because
    He Who promises is Faithful.

He will *never* lie to you.

He will *never* leave you nor forsake you.

He will *never* cast you out of His Hand.

He will *never* forget about you.

He will *never ever* stop Loving you.

He will *never* fail to hear you praying.

He will *never* run out of projects for you to do
    for Him (that's for sure!).

He will *never* give up on you.

He will *never* condemn you.

He will *never* cease to encourage you.

He will *never* lead you down the wrong path.

He will *never* get tired of you.

He will *never* run out of patience with you.

Even now, He is patiently waiting for you to respond to Him. You respond to the Lord through prayer. Praying is simply talking personally with your Heavenly Father through Jesus, His Son. Prayer is the way you express your great love for God *to God*. And it's the way you say "Yes!" to Jesus. If you don't know how to pray to God, don't worry — He knows how to listen. He's good at listening, and He's listening *right now*! You can say whatever is in your heart to say. God *Loves* you so much, and He has been waiting to hear *your* voice for such a long time.

The Lord is looking into your broken, repentant heart and listening to the cry of your soul. If words fail you, just cry, "Lord, be merciful to me ... *the sinner.*" And *He will*! If you will sincerely respond to Jesus' "Call" to you, He will give you a "Response!" And you will *know* that God has shown up in your life. In case you're wondering what *I* said, I'll tell you about it.

"Come and hear, all ye that fear God, and I will declare what He hath done for my soul"

(PSALM 66:16).

According to Pastor James McDonald, "If you don't have a 'conversion story,' you don't have a conversion." I love to hear people "give their testimony" and tell how the Lord "Saved" them. I'm praying that *you* will soon have your own "conversion story" of God's Saving Power!

I was not raised in a Godly home. So, at the age of thirty-one, I had essentially never gone to Church or read the Bible. Really! I was living *in* the world, and I was *of* the world. God was nowhere on my radar. *But*, Praise the Lord, *I* was on *HIS*! He sent the Hounds of Heaven after me before I ever knew Him. Little did I know ... He *already* knew *me*! He Loved me 'ere I knew Him.

The "Hound" He sent after me appeared as a total stranger who just walked up to me (several times) in a public place and *finally* got the chance to tell this lost soul about Jesus and His so Great Salvation! Since I had never been a Churchgoer or read the Bible, he may as well have been speaking a foreign language. I was clueless. His words were in English, but my soul was in such darkness that I just couldn't grasp their meaning. However, when God is in it, He gets His work done.

That faithful servant of God invited this lost worldling to a Christian Ministry he knew about. But I would never have gone ... *except that* in the Providence of God, He had arranged for me to be in a very "dark place" in the already dark, lost life I was living.

It's really true: God will grease the tracks in whichever direction you decide to go, and *I* had decided to go in the opposite direction of God. But now, out of desperation, I decided to give in and go. To say that I was being gloriously "set up" by the God of this Universe would be an understatement ... because when I showed up, He was already there – waiting for me.

I don't remember a thing said during the service, other than a song and some words spoken by the members of the singing group. But *nothing* could penetrate my stone-cold-dead soul. *However,* during the closing prayer, with my head bowed and my eyes closed, the Lord Jesus revealed Himself to me in a surprisingly powerful way.

It began when I suddenly "sensed" a *Presence* with me ... convicting me of the ungodly life I was living. A frightening darkness filled my soul like a murky black fog, and I could hear *Someone* telling me that I was on my way to *hell*! What?! At that point in my life, hell was just a joke. But *somehow* I knew it was true. God's Holy Spirit was working on me before I even knew He existed. *Mercy Me!* (Yeah, that's what I needed.)

A dark, foreboding feeling of horror and terror seized me. I had never felt so helpless, so hopeless, so lost, and so fearful as I did at *that moment*! People who don't fear hell have never gotten a taste of it. I suddenly *knew* that hell would be my eternal place of punishment when I died. *But God* is full of Mercy and Compassion, and I sensed the *Presence* still with me. I *just knew* that I wasn't alone.

Then, even though I was fully conscious, I felt as if – in some amazing way – I was being drawn into ... what I can only describe as ... a *very real dream*!

Don't ask me to explain how it happened. I can't. But in my mind's-eye, I was suddenly standing at the foot of a tall wooden Cross. I sensed a Man's Presence on that Cross, so I looked up at Him. And when I did, wouldn't you know ... He was looking straight at *me*! Our eyes locked, and in that moment I could *feel* floods and floods of Divinely Pure Love passing from His Spirit into mine – through those Eyes of Love. I had never felt "Love" like *that* before in my life!

(**NOTE:** If you watch Ian McCormack's Original Testimony, you will notice a similarity in our testimonies at this point. Why so similar? Answer: Because the same Lord Who *Saved* me, *Saved* Ian as well. The same Lord Who filled me with His Great Love, filled Ian as well. *Now*, the same Lord Jesus is longing to fill *you* with His Great Love and *Save you* as well. *Now,* it's *your* turn to "let Him!")

No one had to tell me that it was Jesus on that Cross ... I *just knew*. There at the foot of Jesus' Cross, with His Love pouring into my spirit, and His Eyes piercing deeply into my soul, my heart could "hear" His thoughts toward me.

Jesus lovingly called my name, and said, "Molly, I Love you.

I'm dying for you. Look at Me, Molly! I'm doing *this* for *YOU!*"

Wow! And to think, I walked into that place not believing in ... anything. Now here I was, miraculously standing before The God Who knows me *by my name* ... and could surely tell me all things that ever I did! Can you imagine how blown away I was to be so *powerfully* confronted by a God I had never even given much thought to? (Do I know where *you* are, or what?)

Then, deep in my spirit, I could hear Jesus asking me a question. He was asking me a vitally important, life-changing question. He was asking me *the question* ... the question we must *all* answer in order for Jesus to "Save" us.

The Lord lovingly asked, "Molly, will you *let* Me die for you?"

Well, what are you going to say to *this Man*? In my heart of hearts, I *knew* that The One in Whose Divine Presence I now stood was no mere man. "The Man" on that Cross was indeed God's Son ... offering me a Divine Invitation. I was in the Holy Presence of God – Who knows me, Who Loves me, Who was dying for me, and Who was now "Calling" me unto Himself ... and I *knew* it.

"Truly this Man is The Son of God!"

(MARK 15:39).

I couldn't explain it. I couldn't understand it. But I couldn't deny it. I think I know how Mary felt when the Angel Gabriel suddenly appeared to her announcing that *she* would give birth to Jesus. It was all so *unreal* ... and yet, so "Very Real!" So *unbelievable* ... and yet, "I Believed!" Jesus was giving me His Faith to believe even though I had never asked Him to ... the same way Mary had never asked to be the Mother of the Messiah. Jesus seems to *Love* showing up when and where He's least expected.

At that moment, my entire Eternal Destiny was wrapped up

in *one question*: "Molly, will you *let* Me die for you?" I was still trembling from the revelation moments earlier that my sin was condemning me to an eternal death. I *knew* that I needed Jesus to *Save* me more than I had ever known anything.

So, from the very depths of my being, my heart cried out, "**YES!**" It was not audible. No one around me heard a word. It was all between my Lord and me, as I said "I Do!" to my Heavenly Bridegroom. In one *glorious moment*, our hearts locked, and I became the Betrothed Bride of Jesus Christ!

Tears of Joy streamed down my face as Heaven's King took my frail hand with His strong nail-pierced Hand ... and a Divine Journey with "The Love of my Life" began. Our Marriage will one day be consummated in Heaven. Until then, my Lord and I are on a "Lifetime Adventure" of walking together through His world. We freely and joyously give those He came to Save the Best News ever – His Glorious Gospel, the Power of God unto Salvation to *all* who believe! But that's another story for another time. For now, let's get back to you. What did *you* say?

It's time for you to "call on Jesus from your heart." He will hear you (Romans 10:13). In fact, He *has* heard your cry, "Jesus, Son of God, have *mercy* on me!" And Jesus is standing still. Time is standing still as Jesus is calling for *you*!

So, be of good comfort. Arise! Cast off your filthy rags and come to Jesus ... just as you are. He calleth thee! And He's been expecting you for such a long time. In fact, He has some new clothes for you – the White Robe of The Righteousness of Christ!

If you want to know for sure that God is Real and has the Power to Save you, just call on Him from your heart ... the very depths of your soul. Say to Him those words He's longing to hear:

*"Lord, I have sinned against You, and I'm
lost – for all Eternity!*

Please forgive me, Lord.

I know now that Jesus is Your Son, and He died for me!

*Wash all my sins away with Jesus'
Precious Blood.*

Thank You, Lord Jesus, for dying for me.

*I trust You, Lord, as my Saviour.
Yes, I receive You – right now.*

*SAVE me, Lord! Right this moment!
Save ME!*

*Fill me with Your Holy Spirit! And I will never
ever be ashamed of You, Lord.
I promise.*

*In the Mighty Name of Jesus,
Amen."*

Then, He will open your blind eyes like He did Bartimaeus', and you will be able to actually "see" His Marvelous Light, deeply "feel" His Glorious Love, and joyously "live" His Divine Life!

*"For whosoever shall call
upon the Name of The Lord
shall be Saved!"*

(ROMANS 10:13)

Today, while the Lord gives you breath, use it to say "Yes!" to Jesus ... at last. Then, you will finally know why Born-Again Christians are so in love with Jesus, and why we do such "strange" things for our Lord. In Jesus' World, where He's waiting for you, not only does Jesus Love *you*, but you love

Him with all your heart. When your heart and His Heart are knit together, you can take anything ole slewfoot throws at you from *his* world ... knowing that you can never lose Jesus' Love!

Do you want to enter Jesus' Divine World? It's just a heart-beat away. However, the ole accuser of the Brethren, satan, keeps bringing up all your sins. Fortunately for you, the Best Defense Attorney in the Universe is pleading your case. Jesus Christ, your Advocate and your Defender, is the Judge's Son! So, you've got it made.

Listen! Your Attorney is giving you some advice. It sounds good.

Jesus is saying, "Let Me die for you! It's your only chance."

I believe that the missing link to Salvation for many people is that little word "let." I talk to lots of folks who know the Gospel perfectly ... but they have never been "Saved." As I probe the problem, I discover that they are usually Church-goers who believe in God, believe in Jesus and know that He died on the Cross for the sins of the world. *But*, when I ask, "Have you ever let Jesus die for *you*?" ... they freeze. They think for a minute, and then slowly shake their head "no."

Jesus doesn't want *you* to be like those folks. He wants you to know the Truth: He has *already* died for you. Now, all *you* have to do is "let Him!" Right here! Right now! Just say "YES!" to Jesus Christ – your Lord, your Saviour, your Heavenly Bride-groom, *and* your Divine Defense Attorney. Take Attorney Jesus' wise counsel. Let Him die for *you*. Let His Precious Blood wash you clean of every sin. It will be the *Best Decision* you ever made, and the *Best Thing* you ever did. You'll see.

Listen closely, and you will hear Jesus' still small Voice asking, "Will you let Me die for you?" Respond to Him from deep in your heart. Don't turn down the Best Offer you've ever had in your whole life. No! Your entire Eternal Destiny is hanging in the balance!

So, what will you say to Jesus' Divine Proposal?

Over the centuries, men have come up with all kinds of creative and unusual ways to propose to their future bride. But none can even come close to the way *our* Heavenly Bridegroom did it. He managed to get a bunch of obsessed evil men to arrest Him in the middle of the night, illegally convict Him of made-up crimes, mercilessly beat Him, cruelly crown Him with a crown of thorns, then nail Him to a wooden Cross to die. On that Cross Jesus bowed His knee and showed His Great Love for His Beloved.

The Words of Jesus from the Cross that are *still* being spoken today are, "Will you marry Me?"

So, will you? He's patiently waiting for your answer to His Divine Proposal. The Lord of everything in the Universe lacks one thing – your heart. And only you can give it to Him.

Johnny Cash proposed to his future bride, June Carter, in the middle of a large concert one night. As June protested, tried to ignore him and desperately tried to keep the song going, Johnny just kept asking her over and over, "Will you marry me?" The entire audience was chanting, "Say 'Yes!' Say 'Yes!' Say 'Yes!'" Finally, June was so overcome with emotion and love that she gave in to her heart's desire and said, "Yes!"

Now, what about you? If you are still protesting, ignoring Jesus and desperately trying to keep your life going without Him, you need to stop for a minute and listen closely. At this moment, in the *Spiritual Realm*, you are surrounded by so great a cloud of witnesses: The Father, the Bridegroom (Jesus), The Holy Spirit, the Angels and the Saints – *ALL* praying, "Say 'YES!' Say 'YES!' Say 'YES!'"

So, what is your answer to Jesus? Multitudes, multitudes in the valley of decision. When are *you* going to give up and give in to your heart's desire? You will never know how *abundantly full* your life can be … until you say "YES!" to Jesus.

"Come and see the Works of God!"

(PSALM 66:5).

Is a battle going on in your soul? Does satan have your number and the price is right? It's been said that every man has his price, but don't *you* sell-out to the devil. If you do, you'll end up paying *him* a price that is *Eternally* way *too high*! Sell-out to Jesus. *He* has paid the highest Price of all for you – *His Life*!

The satan-filled life is a dead-end street. It ends up in hell … *forever*! But the Jesus-filled life is an Eternity of glorious, everlasting Joy! Go for The Gold. Go for the glorious Joy … *forever*!

"Unto Him be Glory in the Church by Christ Jesus throughout all Ages, World without end. Amen."

(EPHESIANS 3:21)

Maybe you're listening to your unbelieving friends who are telling you that the Resurrection of Jesus Christ was all a hoax, a fake, a staged conspiracy. They're laughing and telling you that *no one* can come back from the dead. And they are right. *No one* can come back from the dead … *but God*!

So, let me ask you this, "If your friends are right, and Jesus isn't God, and He didn't come out of that tomb … then Who was that 'Man' Who *Supernaturally* appeared to me and *Powerfully* changed my heart, my soul, my mind, my life, and my Destiny – *forever*! Who took all my sin, my guilt, my fear, my sorrow, my depression, my doubt, and my turmoil, and gave me His Amazing Love, His Great Joy, His Deep Peace, His Godly Wisdom, and His constant Companionship? Who gives me *Spiritual* eyes to see Heaven and my King upon His Throne? Who fills my days with Thanksgiving and Praise to The God of my Salvation? Is it any wonder that my life-verse is II Timothy 1:12?

> *'For the which cause I also suffer these things;*
> *nevertheless I am not ashamed,*
> *for I know Whom I have believed*
> *and am persuaded that He is able*
> *to keep that which I have committed*
> *unto Him against that day!'"*

II TIMOTHY 1:12:

So, Who *was* that Divinely Supernatural "Man"? What is your explanation?

You see, a man with a totally transformed life is never at the mercy of a man with an argument. You're arguing with God, and you are bound to lose. So, just go ahead and lose. Take a Godly tip: Surrender to God. Die to yourself and your pride and let the Resurrected Christ resurrect *you*! When you do, you will discover that the True Christian Life is the "Power of Jesus' Resurrected Life" being lived out of *you*!

Whenever satan's crowd announces they've found the bones of Jesus (Oh, my!), it doesn't rattle me in the least. I know beyond any doubt that Jesus is *Alive* and well ... in *me*. So, I don't worry about whatever bones *they* 'claim' to have ... because I know that Jesus isn't lacking any bones today – He has *mine*!

Now is the time for us to revisit Jesus' bold proclamation: "All that The Father giveth Me shall come to Me!"

So ... has God given you to His Son, Jesus? Have you discovered the answer yet? There is only one way you will ever find out. Come and see!

> There is Hope in just one look at Jesus on the Cross.
>
> There is Life in just one drop of the Blood of The Lamb.
>
> There is Joy in just one tear of The Man of sorrows.
>
> There is Peace in just one touch of the nail-pierced Hand of The Christ of Calvary.
>
> It all begins at the foot of Jesus' Eternal Cross. What are you waiting for? *He's* still waiting for you!

"Let him who is athirst come. And whosoever will, let him take the Water of Life freely!"

(REVELATION 22:17).

"The proof is in the pudding." Ever heard that? Do you know what it means? Yeah, it doesn't make any sense, does it?

"Just come to Jesus, and He will *Save* you." Ever heard someone say *that*? Yep, and you didn't know what that meant either.

Well, the original ole proverb actually says, "The proof of the pudding is in the eating thereof."

Aha! You've got to eat the pudding to find out if it's good, or not. Same with Jesus. It takes more than just coming to

Jesus and looking at Jesus for Him to *Save* you. You come to Jesus deep in your soul ... because that's where all "Spiritual Transactions" between Jesus and you take place. The Lord promises that if you will seek Him with *all your heart*, you will find Him. As you seek Him in prayer, you will sense Him looking at *you* (spiritually speaking). That's when you confess your sin to Him, ask His forgiveness and *receive Him* into your spirit. You must open your heart's door and *take Jesus into* your inner-man. That's when you find out how good and how sweet Jesus really is. The proof of your Christianity is in the *very real* Presence of Jesus the Christ in *you*!

"If any man thirst, let him come unto Me and drink!"
Signed: Jesus

(JOHN 7:37).

I am so thankful to my Heavenly Father that He drew me to His Son's Cross years ago. As I stood there in judgment before Him, I humbly agreed with Him that I was guilty as charged: A lost sinner on my way to hell for all Eternity. He then granted me His Great Mercy and gave me His Grace to believe that Jesus *is* The Messiah – the Saviour Who died for *me*! I just needed to *let* Him. And when I did, the Light went on, and I could see the Truth: *I* was the guilty one who should have been crucified – not the innocent Son of God. It should have been *me* who had to hang on that Cross in shame and disgrace. But, with Holy Love pouring out of every pore of His ravaged body, my Gracious Saviour took *my* place there! What can I do but say "Thank You, Lord!"? I'll tell you what else I can do. I can tell *you* that Jesus is taking *your* place there too.

"O the Love that drew Salvation's Plan!

O the Grace that brought it down to man!

O the mighty gulf that God did span ... at Calvary!

Mercy there was great, and Grace was free,

Pardon there was multiplied to me,

There my burdened soul found liberty ... at Calvary!"

(WILLIAM NEWELL)

"I'm so unworthy of such Mercy, but I know that when Jesus was on that Cross, I was on His Mind!"

(JASON CRABB).

Now, what about you? What do *you* know? Are you tired of living but scared of dying? The day that you finally wake up and say, "There has to be a better way" will be the first time in your life you were right – Eternally right! May this Jesus-sent book be Jesus' alarm clock in your heart.

However, you may be the skeptic who says, "You Christians don't deal with reality."

Oh, really? Is your life on Earth real? Is your soul real? Is your love/joy/hope/fear/sorrow/hate/pain real? Are your thoughts real? Is your death real? Of course, they are. And I'll tell you what else is real –

God is Real!

You see, *Faith* isn't blind. Oh no, Faith is responding with eyes that have been opened wide by the True and Living God to His *very real* Personal Presence. Are you breathing? You will take your next breath because Jesus Christ graciously gives it to you ... in a body He has miraculously provided for you.

I know God exists because He interrupted my life with a "Divine Revelation" of Himself and His Great Love for *me.* Today, I love *Him*, and He lets me *know* that He is with me in ways both seen and unseen. His Love for me unfolds at each new bend in the road of life.

God loves you too. He has been *loving you* and *calling to you* over the siren-call of this evil world *all your life*. The Lord Jesus is loving you and calling to you right now ... *and you know it.* I rest my case.

Maybe you're the guy who thinks that God might really exist, *but* you're just going to wait and take your chances with Him when you die. Not a good plan. In the final analysis, all sins are against God. That means you are indebted to God for every sin you've ever committed (*plus* Adam's original sin which you were stuck with when you were born).

> *"And God is going to throw the Book at you — the Bible!"*
>
> (MATT FOX).

So, let me ask you this, "What can you give God to persuade Him to let sinful you into His Holy Heaven? What do you have that you can offer God in exchange for your Salvation?"

You say, "All my good works."

Sorry, Charlie, but you're living under a delusion. *God* says,

> *"The soul that sinneth, it shall die"*
>
> (EZEKIEL 18:20).

So, if you have ever committed even one sin, you are living under God's curse. And *He's* not going to be impressed with "all your good works" ... because they will *never* cancel out the curse you're living under due to your sin (plus the *Big One* you inherited from your Forevermore-Great-Granddaddy Adam).

And while you're thinking about how innocent you are, consider this: Your sin (ever so small) *still* cost God the sacrifice of His Precious Son, Jesus. Yep. So, tell me again how much you *don't* owe God.

Sad to say, but you've got *nothing* on your resume that would ever justify you before the God of Glory. So *now,* whatcha gonna try?

You say, "I'll declare to God that I'm not guilty by reason of 'temptation.' I just couldn't resist all those 'tempting things' everywhere I looked!" *(Hmmm).*

Sounds to me like you're blaming the devil. Well, Adam and Eve already tried that one – and it didn't work for them either. (Actually, Adam blamed Eve, Eve blamed the serpent, and the serpent didn't have a leg to stand on.)

Got any other clever ideas? I hate to have to tell you this, but you are spiritually bankrupt! The only thing you really have, spiritually speaking, is your sin. Just admit it: Your goose is cooked, your number is up, and *you* don't have a leg to stand on either. Your only hope is to settle with God out of Court ... at all costs!

So, just go ahead and give God what you have. Confess it all to the God Who knows all about you, loves you anyway and died Himself to pay the penalty for all your sins (and mine too). The path to Spiritual Salvation is Spiritual bankruptcy. O happy day, happy day, when you finally realize how spiritually poor you are, and how spiritually rich God's Son is. Only Jesus will do for you what you could never do for yourself. It's called: God's Love through His Grace (or God's Grace through His Love).

So, give God your sin and let Him put it *all* on His Son, Jesus. Then, Jesus will take your filthy sins, wash them away with His Precious Blood and give you His White Robe of Righteousness as your own! You won't be perfect, but you *will* be "Perfectly Forgiven!" You will be eternally sorry if you don't make this trade. You can't run from the Lord … so run to Him!

> *"All roads lead to God …*
> *but not all roads lead to Heaven"*
>
> ─────────
> (GREG LAURIE).

God has a Divine Plan for Planet Earth. Would you like to help Him "work His Plan"? Do you have any desire to be included? Truth is, you *are* included … either for good or for ill – you chose. Presently, you are choosing to help satan work *his* plan on Earth. *But God* desires to use you to *defeat* satan and his evil agenda.

Therefore, the Lord must first defeat satan's power over *you.* God didn't send you to this Earth to just draw your breath, draw your paycheck, draw your retirement … then die and draw your family to the reading of your Will to draw what you didn't.

No! God sent you here to draw your breath as you draw close to Him through Jesus, His Son. Then, draw attention to Jesus, draw folks to Him with your witness, draw a myriad of lost people into God's Kingdom … then die and draw your Eternal Reward from Jesus for *all Eternity.* Forget earthly toys … he who dies with *Jesus* as his Saviour WINS! *Mercy Me!*

If you are one of the young Folks, you are so amazing. You have all that energy, and you *think* you know what to do with it. But you just don't know what *the Lord Jesus* would do with it … *if* He could get you and all your youthful energy working for *His* Kingdom instead of satan's.

However, satan wants to keep you working for him in *his* kingdom. So, when Christians like me try telling you about Jesus, your boss gives you the perfect answer, "I'm good."

Yep, you're good alright. When you belong to satan, you aren't good for nothing. Oh no, you are very good for your master, satan, and his evil agenda on Planet Earth. But the truth is, the most exciting life in the world isn't being a powerful politician, a glamorous movie star, a rock star, a sports star, or a famous "somebody" with lots of money, cars, mansions, babes (guys), jets, jewels, fame, etc. Nope, the most exciting life in the whole world is getting to tell lost people (who belong to satan) about the Glorious Saviour, Jesus, Who can set them free from their demonic addictions to this sin-cursed world and give them a Home in Heaven for all Eternity when they die. *That* is what excites *Jesus.* And when Jesus is happy, everybody's happy ... even *you*!

Now, I know what you're thinking, "You're saying such strange things ... I think that you're just ... 'mentally challenged'." (Otherwise known as crazy.)

May I reveal to you God's Truth: Only a Born-Again Christian is truly in their right mind. I think better, feel better, "see" better, talk better, live better and definitely behave better than I ever did before the Lord graciously "Saved" me. And trust me, so will you! *But you* are willfully choosing to follow satan (who is taking you to hell with him *forever*) when the Lord is offering you "The Way" to belong to Him and go to Heaven with *Him forever*! And you say *I'm* mentally challenged. *(Hmmm).*

"Then they went out ... and found the man, out of whom the devils were departed, sitting at the feet of Jesus, clothed and in his right mind"

(LUKE 8:35).

One of the hardest decisions to make in life is deciding which bridge to burn and which bridge to cross. So, let me "be Jesus" to you right now and give you some Godly advice. The Cross of Jesus Christ is The Bridge to God, to Heaven, and to Eternal Life! *That* is The Bridge you need to cross in your life *today*. Don't wait another minute to take that first step. Take The Bridge that will hold the weight of all your sin.

> *"Accepting Jesus as your Saviour isn't a*
> *twelve-step program ... it's a one-step program"*
>
> (GREG LAURIE).

You may be wondering how "Jesus being born in me" is going to happen. Well, you aren't alone. Mary, the Mother of Jesus, asked the Angel Gabriel the same question when he announced to her that she was going to conceive a child. He answered her with these words,

> *"The Holy Ghost shall come upon thee,*
> *and the Power of The Highest shall overshadow thee:*
> *therefore also that Holy One Who shall be*
> *born of thee shall be called The Son of God"*
>
> (LUKE 1:35).

And that is exactly what happened. In a mysteriously Divine way, God the Spirit fathered God the Son in Mary' womb!

At the moment you trust Jesus as your Saviour and God Saves *you*, His Holy Spirit enters your spirit and gives birth to "Jesus' Spirit" in *your* spirit. Jesus is "Born Again" in *you*! God's Spirit uses *your body* to give Birth to the Spirit of God's Son on Earth. The really glorious thing about His conception in *you* is that He won't be leaving you in nine months. Like Mary, you are so very blessed, and in a way, Jesus is closer to you than He was to Mary. Jesus was in Mary's womb. When He is Born-Again in you, He is in your *very spirit* … forever! The God of your Salvation is Supernatural, and so is your Salvation!

> *"That if thou shalt confess*
> *with thy mouth the Lord Jesus,*
> *and shalt believe in thine heart*
> *that God hath raised Him from the dead,*
> *thou shalt be Saved!"*

(ROMANS 10:9).

If you said "YES!" to Jesus like I did,

"WELCOME TO HIS WORLD!"

Now, Galatians 2:20 is your verse, too:

> *"I am crucified with Christ, nevertheless I live:*
> *yet not I, but Christ liveth in me;*
> *and the life which I now live in the flesh,*
> *I live by the Faith of the Son of God,*
> *Who loved me, and gave Himself for me!"*

GALATIANS 2:20

> *See, I told you that you were going to be crucified …*
> *but that's good! The "old you" had to die*
> *so that the "New You" can live.*
> *And what is the "New You"?*
> *It's "Christ in you," the Hope of Glory*

(COLOSSIANS 1:27).

Aha! **CHRIST IN YOU!** Now *you* can dare to "be Jesus" on this Earth — He's Living right inside of you! You are a chosen vessel unto the Lord, and you are no longer just a "man of the flesh." When you let Jesus die for you, not only did Christ's Spirit enter your spirit, but your spirit entered Christ's Spirit. Therefore, you were "in Christ" when He was on that Cross ... and your "flesh-life" died with *His* body of flesh. *But Jesus* arose from that tomb! And today, He lives His "Resurrected Spiritual Life" in *your spirit*! The Saviour Who was born in Bethlehem has been *Born-Again* in *you*, my Christian Friend!

Jesus will also live *through* you ... *when you let Him.* And when you do, He will make you more "Alive" than you have ever been in your whole life! At last, you know the Truth: Jesus is God, and *He Arose*! Jesus is *Alive*! And *now*, He's Alive in *you*! Jesus' Presence within you is your power, your joy, your peace, your wisdom, and your reason to live your life as a Christian.

In fact, now that Jesus is your Life, His goal is to make *you* as *alive* as He is ... to God the Father. You have an "Open Door" to Heaven like you've never had before! You no longer have to crash through doors to get what you want. Nope, Jesus has the Keys, and He will open the doors for you ... that He wants you to go through. "Thank You, Lord."

So, just go ahead and have a funeral for yourself and let your Lord Jesus Live in you instead. You will soon discover that "Jesus in you" will be free to live *through you* only to the extent that you are willing to die to yourself and your immoral desires. *Freedom* for the Christian is being free to live your life to please The One Who purchased you with His own Blood. Jesus tells us to take up our cross and follow Him (Matthew 16:24). So, *we* must do the taking up. You will never truly "live" until you carry Jesus' Cross ... with *you* on it. *Mercy Me!*

OLE SLEWFOOT

*"Becoming a Christian costs you nothing ...
being a Christian costs you everything!"*

(GREG LAURIE).

The God Who touched you and Saved you is telling you how much *Jesus Loves you* as you read these words. Jesus has been "Born Again" in you (your spirit-man), and a *Supernatural Transaction* has taken place. Light has dispelled darkness. Truth has destroyed lies. Love has replaced hate. Faith has driven out doubt. Peace has overcome fear. Jesus, God's Son, has won the *Victory* over satan – *forever*!

In Jesus' World, satan has been banished, and Jesus reigns as King upon His Throne! Jesus, and Jesus alone, is fit to take the Universe's Throne. And He alone is fit to sit upon the throne of *your heart.* He is taking His rightful place on the throne of your heart right now. Jesus' Kingdom comes to Earth within every Christian who receives Him as King. Then, His Kingdom goes every place you go.

Jesus is KING! Satan's crowd can't impeach Him, and He is never going to resign – so just go ahead and crown Him KING of *your* life! Give Him the Glory due His Name. Say, "Thank You, Lord" and "I Love You, Jesus." Feels good, doesn't it? For the first time in your life, you can see the Light. You can feel the Love. You can say the Words. You can live the Life! You can dare to "be Jesus" to this world He came to redeem.

*"Therefore with Joy shall ye draw
Water out of the Wells of Salvation!"*

(ISAIAH 12:3).

A New Day is dawning. The dawn of the day of discovery is just beginning for you. Life is a *Miracle*! Your body is a "living miracle" of the God Who created you. Now *Jesus* is living in it *with you*. Take care of your body. Don't defile it in *any* way. Get plenty of exercise – run from the devil and walk with God. Start bringing Glory to your Lord, and never be ashamed of Jesus. He wasn't too ashamed to hang on a Cross and die for *you* and for *me*.

The Lord Jesus filled your heart with His Love when He Saved you. Now, if you love your Lord with all of your heart, give Him what He wants with all of *His* Heart. He wants you. No one else will do. He has set His Heart on *you*. Set *your* heart on giving yourself over to The One Who is waiting right there in your heart to take you. Then, He will bring you into His World with Him ... as soon as you give yourself over to Him – wholeheartedly.

"For whosoever will save his life (for himself) shall lose it, and whosoever will lose his life (you must will it so) for My sake shall find it."
Signed: Jesus

(MATTHEW 16:25).

"God uses serious Christians to do Great Works!"

(PETER MARSHAL, JR.).

So, submit yourself to the mighty Hand of the Lord, and He will direct your steps. When you belong to God, you are one of His "called-out-ones." And as Adrian Rogers says,

"God's Plan for your life is not a roadmap – it's a Relationship!"

Christians of yesteryear used to sing an ole hymn which says that when we die and go to Heaven, we shall see Jesus "Face to face." Well, my Friend, now that you are a Born-Again Christian, *you* know Jesus "Face to face" on this Earth ... in your spirit. The Lord Jesus is right there with you *always,* and He has "Big Plans" for you – always. He is performing an on-going Miracle in your soul to enlarge your heart, expand your mind and open your eyes to see that He is writing a "Magnificent Symphony" with *your life.* Really!

> *"For the Eyes of The Lord run to and fro throughout the whole Earth to show Himself strong in the behalf of them whose heart is perfect toward Him"*

(II CHRONICLES 16:9).

> *"God can take a dedicated Christian with a clear message and change the world!"*

(DAVID JEREMIAH).

Why don't *you* be a Dwight L. Moody and purpose in your heart to *be that man*!

> *"Expect great things from God, attempt great things for God"*

(WILLIAM CAREY).

Now you know the answer to the dilemma of how you can choose not to sin. There is a "New Life" in you, and His Name is Jesus. Jesus has taken up residence in your spirit, bringing with Him God's *Supernatural Love.* This enables you to love Him with His own Divine Love. *Now* you are able to love Jesus enough to let *Him* make your choices for you – and Jesus always chooses righteousness over sin.

Whenever your flesh over-rules your love for your Lord and chooses sin over Him, it will come between you and The One you love. And it will break your heart ... until you yield to Him once again. So, even if you're battling a sinful addiction that you can't seem to defeat, just keep on loving Jesus a little more every day ... until you love *Jesus* more than you love your sin. When you find yourself loving your Lord in your heart enough to hate sin, you will *know* that *Jesus* is "Living" in your spirit. Jesus doesn't want to just be your Saviour. His desire is to be *The Passion* of your soul!

"That the trial of your Faith, being much more precious than of gold that perisheth, though it be tried with fire, might be found unto Praise and Honor and Glory at the appearing of Jesus Christ: Whom having not seen, ye love; in Whom, though now ye see Him not, yet believing, ye rejoice with Joy unspeakable and full of Glory: Receiving the end of your Faith, even the Salvation of your souls"

(I PETER 1:7-9).

"Henceforth I call you not servants, but I have called you friends." Signed: Jesus

(JOHN 15:15).

Now you can call the Lord Jesus your Friend ... because He *is*! In fact, He is your Best Friend. And the man walking with Jesus is going in the right direction ... finally. So, relax. The One Who holds this Universe together can hold your life together. The Lord Jesus upholds you by the Word of His Power! Your job is to thank Him for all things (Ephesians 5:20) and trust Him for His Faithfulness to you each day.

"O give thanks unto The Lord, for He is good; for His Mercy endureth forever!"

(PSALM 118:29).

Take a deep Spiritual breath and *rejoice*! *Now*, "YOU ARE FORGIVEN" of *all* your sins. You are now a Masterpiece of God's Mercy and a Miracle of God's Grace! You can never lose Jesus' Love for you or His Presence within you. Jesus calls the Blood that He shed for you on the Cross: The Blood of the New Covenant. God and you are now in Covenant together. As you read God's Word, He will give you the wisdom to know His part and your part.

The Good News is that *now* you belong to the Lord Jesus. The bad news is that satan is *not* going to give you up without a fight. So, be on guard. Put God's Son, God's Word, and God's People between you and ole slewfoot. Read your Bible every day. It's time you took the "Good Book" and took a good look at the Good God Who gave His Precious Son, Jesus, for *you*! Treasure God's Word. It's His special Gift to you. Read it and let your Lord open His Supernatural World up to *you*. As you read your Bible, "Jesus in you" will thrill to the Words He wrote as His Love Letter to *you*. So, you can be sure … your name is on every page! And so is *His*!

When you read God's Word and it comes *Alive* in your soul, you will *know* that *Jesus* is "Living" in your spirit. And remember, you aren't "just reading a book." Oh no, you're "meeting with a Person" – a Supernatural Person Who is Living right there on the inside of you … meeting with *you*!

"Have Christ always in view when you are reading the Word of God, and this, like the Star in the East, will guide you to the Messiah and unlock to you the wisdom and riches of all the mysteries of the Kingdom of God"

(REV. GEORGE WHITEFIELD).

Mark Twain once said,

"Be careful about reading too many health books – you may die of a misprint."

MOLLY MCCOY

Well, let me assure you on your Lord's behalf: You will never die of a misprint reading your Bible. I know for sure that the Bible is true and reliable because I know for sure that I *know* The One Who wrote it. And I know for sure that *He* is Faithful and True. And now, you know for sure that *you* know Him too! You finally realize that you aren't a Christian because you go to Church or read the Bible. You're a Christian because you *know* The One Who wrote the Bible, and you know for sure that *He knows you*!

"Thou hast both seen Him,
and it is He Who talketh with thee"
said Jesus

(JOHN 9:37).

Listen for the still small Voice of Jesus speaking to you through His Word. As you read God's Truth, Jesus (The Living Word) gives "Life" to your spirit-man. There is a *Supernatural* reason that the Bible is the best-selling Book in the world. There is Power in the Word of God because there is so much Power in the God of the Word.

You can stand confidently on God's Word. It is wholly sufficient for this world and the world which is to come. There is a ton of factual information proving the *miraculous* accuracy of the Bible. God's Truth is a very valuable Revelation in a culture that has made relativism, pluralism, humanism, naturalism, tolerance, and political correctness their 'gods.'

"Thy Word is a Lamp unto my feet,
and a Light unto my path"

(PSALM 119:105).

Face The Son and feel the fresh winds of tomorrow blowing through your soul. Let your dreams be greater than your memories and be willing to let go of your past so that you can grasp with both hands your glorious future! You may have grown up with an abusive, unloving father who mistreated you in the worst way. Your relationship with him may have been (and may still be) sadly bad. But don't dwell on that anymore, because *now, the God of this Universe* is your Father! Can you believe it? Well, believe it ... because *He is*! And *God Loves* you *perfectly.*

> *"The price paid for something determines its value;*
> *and nobody but nobody paid a higher Price for you*
> *than God did when He reached into His wallet*
> *and pulled out His Son, JESUS CHRIST!"*

(TONY EVANS).

> *"Forasmuch as ye know that ye were not redeemed*
> *with corruptible things, as silver and gold ...*
> *but with the Precious Blood of Christ!"*

(I PETER 1:18-19).

In Love, your Heavenly Father "Saves" you just the way you are. But His Love won't leave you the way He found you. Oh no, He is going to spend the rest of your life working on you ... but not to restore you to "Adam before he sinned." Nope, better than that. God is going to spend the rest of your life conforming you to the Image of His Son, Jesus! And if you don't think that's going to take a lot of work, then you're in for an education.

Your Heavenly Father will steadily, tenaciously, gently and as surely as He is on His Throne make you just like His Son, Jesus. And He will *never* give up on you. There will be days you will want to give up on yourself – *but God* won't let you. God's Love is a Love that will not let you go.

Your Lord will never send you back to the devil and say, "Hey, satan, *this* one is just too much trouble. Here! You can have *him* back. Good riddance!"

Never! So, you may as well just be *Thankful*, be *Joyful* and get with *God's* Program. And no matter how many doubts you may have about yourself ... *never* doubt God's great Love for you. All you have to do is just look again toward Calvary to see God's Love being poured out ... for *you*.

When you said "Yes!" to the Lord, you fell on The Rock of your Salvation ... and were broken. You had to be broken ... in order for Him to make you whole. Now, whatever it takes, God will transform you until He can once again see "The Image of God" in *you*. That Image came back at the moment of your Salvation – the moment Christ's Spirit entered into your spirit. Now, He is slowly, gently, wisely and methodically getting rid of all those things in you that blur His Image.

God may even have to send you into the furnace of affliction in order for The Refiner's fire to burn all that dross off of your gold! That's because you're the guy who doesn't change when you see The Light ... but only when you feel the heat. So, just go ahead and co-operate with The Refiner, and it will be a whole lot less painful. Then, the day will come when you can see that your Lord didn't Save you to make you always happy ... but to make you *His*, so that He can live His Life *in* you and *through* you – always with great Joy!

"Happiness is something you stumble over on your way to serve Jesus!"

(ADRIAN ROGERS).

Gladly render unto God the things that are God's. That would be you, by the way, because *you* bear "The Image of God." Soon you will be glorifying God and enjoying Him forever! And you will discover a wonderful truth: You will never have a greater treasure in all of life than Jesus Himself. Jesus *Living* His Supernatural Life in you *Personally* is the "Abundant Life" He promises you. So, be prepared to be amazed at what your Lord is going to do *through you*. He wants *you* to see in you all that *He* sees in you.

> *"Behold, the eye of The Lord*
> *is upon them that fear Him,*
> *upon them that hope in His Mercy"*

(PSALM 33:18).

As you walk with your Lord, you may stumble and fall. If you do, confess your sin to Him and thank Him for His faithfulness to wash all your sin away with His Precious Blood.

> *"'Fess up, free up,*
> *lighten up and Live!*
> *Live like you're going to*
> *live forever because you are!"*

(KEN DAVIS).

Then, your Strong Saviour will pick you up, brush you off and put you back in *The Race*. Jesus fixes you up and puts you back in business – the Business of His Kingdom Work. It is always better to fail seeking to do the Will of God than to succeed doing the will of satan. You've had a bellyful of that rascal, and you're done with *his* evil agenda.

MOLLY MCCOY

"The Lord upholdeth all that fall,
and raiseth up all those that be bowed down"

(PSALM 145:14).

"The God of this Universe has a plan for your life.
You can try, but you cannot stop God's Plan for you.
Your failures don't mean that God has failed.
God will still work out His Plan"

(JEFF WICKWIRE).

Pray and ask your Lord to make you better than you used to be so that your tomorrows will be better than your yesterdays. And He will! The Lord will strengthen you in your "inner-man" with all might according to His Glorious Power. Jesus' little Lambs are weak ... but we have a Strong Shepherd Who is ready to help at the sound of the weakest "baaaaaaaaaa."

The longer you walk with your Lord, the more you will realize how much you need Him ... for everything. And may I reveal something else to you that most Christians seem to miss? I know it sounds strange, but the Lord Jesus needs *us*! The powerful God of this Universe needs *you*. His Big Plan to build His Church depends on little you ... and little me. The "life" of one man's soul depends on the words of another ... who is depending on Jesus to help him help *Him* add to His Church daily such as should be "Saved."

You may have come to Jesus as a gang member (or even as a gang leader like Nicky Cruz). So, you'll be happy to hear that *now* you can join "The Jesus Revolution!" But calm down ... you won't be carrying guns and knives. Nope, you'll be "packin' heat" alright, *but* it will be the Love of Jesus in your heart and the Gospel of Christ on your lips. And *those* are the most Powerful Weapons on Earth! So, you will definitely be armed and dangerous ... to satan and his demons. Now it's time to get busy forming your own "Band of Jesus' Joyful Men." Take from the evil one and give them to the Lord – Who is going forth to overcome the world ... through *you*. *Mercy Me!*

"I've always thought that the most powerful weapon
in the world was the (nuclear) bomb ...
but I've come to the conclusion that
the most powerful weapon
in the world is not the bomb ...
it is the truth."

(ANDREI SAKHAROV).

All the great Christians of the past served God in their generation. Now, they have passed the baton of the Gospel into *your* hands, and you are accountable to your Lord for what *you* do with it. *This* is *your* chance! Start praying "Big Prayers" to the God of Heaven – like Nehemiah did. Then, expect your Lord to use *you* to be the answer to your own prayers.

Case in point: This book. I have been witnessing and praying for *Revival* in America for many years. *And then one day,* I was just sitting there minding my own business, when "Oliver Sutton," out of the Blue (Heaven) ... God put His Hand on *me* to write this book. You just never know ... *but God* knows!

Now it's your turn to attempt "Big Things" for God as you prayerfully seek His guidance. Let the Lord lead you. He is your Shepherd – and He is the Good Shepherd. *Nothing* is impossible with our Great God! *HE* can bring *Revival* to our dark Land ... when we all get with *His* Program. And always stay humble. Never forget that the only reason you are a Child of God is because God the Son was willing to shed His Precious Blood and die for you. You're under "New Management" now. You are no longer "the boss" of your life.

God is always seeking for Himself a man after His own Heart. The Lord is looking for *someone* who will stand in the gap for Him. He's looking for a man who is bold, courageous, confident, and obedient ... like Jesus. He's looking for a man of virtue, integrity, and character – a man of God. Will you purpose in your heart to be that man? *Be that man,* and you will never regret it. If you have come to that place in your life where all you truly have is Jesus Christ, then what do you have to lose?

Even when you *think* you've lost something, your Lord will graciously repay you many times over – either on this Earth or in Heaven. Jesus promises. Now it's your turn to keep *your* promise to *Him* to never be ashamed of Him. You do that by telling people about Him. It's called "witnessing for Jesus," and *that's* what I want to help you do. Jesus calls us to: "Come and see! Go and tell!"

Mark Gregston says that Dads want to fix as much as Moms want to talk. Well, now's your chance, Christian Dad. If you want to fix your Country, your city, your family, and most of all – your kids – take them out witnessing. Oh, yeah! Let them watch you telling lost folks about *Jesus.* It's your job to train them up to take your place after your Lord has taken *you* up to Heaven. Show them what the "Joy of Jesus *in you*" looks like.

And kids, listen up. Are you at odds with your parents? Do you ever get mad at them and rebel? Can a bluebird fly? Well, why is this so?

Answer: Because you want to do (or have) something, and *they won't let you*. Right? Of course.

Now, I hate to have to be the one to ruin your day, but as you grow older, your Heavenly Father is going to refuse you *your* wishes and bring *His* wishes into your life instead – and you aren't going to like it.

So ... you can learn *now* to humble yourself under the authority of your earthly father, *or* your Heavenly Father will bring you to your knees *later* ... as only He can do. Your choice. The sooner you learn this lesson, the sooner you will have the

Peace of God in your life – and in your family.

Now, I know what you're thinking, "But my Dad is way wrong!"

In *your* eyes. In a chapter of my future book *Dare To Be Jesus II*, I recall a time when, as a kid, I was absolutely convinced that *my* Daddy was wrong. However, I have lived to see that he was absolutely *right*. There have even been times when I thought my Heavenly Father was way wrong too. But I just needed time to mature in the Lord ... and so do you.

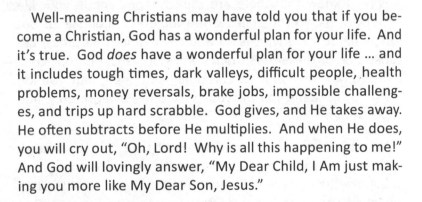

Well-meaning Christians may have told you that if you become a Christian, God has a wonderful plan for your life. And it's true. God *does* have a wonderful plan for your life ... and it includes tough times, dark valleys, difficult people, health problems, money reversals, brake jobs, impossible challenges, and trips up hard scrabble. God gives, and He takes away. He often subtracts before He multiplies. And when He does, you will cry out, "Oh, Lord! Why is all this happening to me!" And God will lovingly answer, "My Dear Child, I Am just making you more like My Dear Son, Jesus."

So, just keep on walking with your Lord, and He will enlighten your *soul* by means of His Presence within your *spirit* ... showing you His Truth of how He works all things together for His Glory and your *Eternal* good. You will start seeing that your Lord is taking you *through* those tough times for the purpose of drawing you closer and closer and closer to Himself. Thank Him. It's worth it all because you're seeing Jesus ... more and more and more. The same Lord Who walked with Daniel's three friends in the fiery furnace is still walking with *you* today. You belong to Jesus now, and He will take care of you.

MOLLY MCCOY

"'Ere He giveth, or He taketh,
God His Children ne'er forsaketh"

(KAROLINA SANDELL-BERG).

God is making you wiser and stronger so that He can use you even better. Your life is being poured out in sacrificial service by your Lord Himself for *His purposes*. God ruthlessly perfects whom He Royally elects. God knows what He's about. The Lord is making you into a *genuine* Christian. According to Adrian Rogers, a hypocritical Christian is someone who has everything in the showcase ... and nothing in the warehouse. Your Lord wants better things for you. So, He's busy stocking *your* storehouse with plenty of His Godly inventory.

Now, I know that there are things happening in your life right now that you don't like ... and you don't understand. But just hang in there with Jesus and trust Him at all times, because one of these days, things will start falling into place ... and you will "see" what He was doing all along. Then, you will pray, "Lord, thank You for your Wisdom, Power, Mercy, and Love. Amen."

When I have two different kinds of fruit to eat, I always eat the less sweet one first. If I eat the sweetest one first, it will make the less sweet one taste bitter. *But,* if I eat the less sweet one first, the sweeter one will taste even sweeter. God does that in our lives. He lets us go through the bitter first, so that the sweet will be even sweeter. "Thank You, Lord."

So, on those dark days when you don't think you can make it up hard scrabble one more time, *Jesus will show up* with the Supernatural Strength His Father gave *Him* to make it up Mount Calvary ... one last time – for *you*. So smile, as you walk on with your hand confidently in the Hand of The Man Who calms the sea ... and you.

OLE SLEWFOOT

*"Fear thou not, for **I AM** with thee;*
I will strengthen thee,
yea, I will help thee; yea,
I will uphold thee with
the Right Hand of My Righteousness"

(ISAIAH 41:10).

Have you been going through your whole life with the elusive feeling that you were always searching for *something* … but you just never could quite find it? Well cheer up, Dear Heart, because that *something* you have been searching for is really "Someone," and He has been relentlessly searching for *you*. Actually, He has been *drawing you* – and now, He has let you find Him. The journey is finally over. It all ended at the foot of the Cross of Jesus Christ.

No! The Journey is just beginning!

"If you have been Heaven-Born …
you are Heaven-Bound!"

(ADRIAN ROGERS).

Now you have a "New Song" to sing, and it's right there within your heart. You can sing "The Song of The Redeemed." Your heart explodes with the Joy of Jesus! Your Wonderful Saviour has broken satan's chains and set you free … at last! His Banners of Love, Mercy, and Grace are flying over your soul … with beams of Eternal Light ever before you.

When the Lord Saved you, He gave you a new *Heart,* a new *Mind*, a new *Life*, new *Eyes*, and new *Ears*. You will never look at life the same again, and you will start hearing the still small Voice of Jesus as He speaks to you deep within your heart. In fact, you may be hearing Him right now saying,

"WELCOME TO MY WORLD!"

NOW YOU KNOW THE ANSWER.

God did indeed give you to His Son, Jesus.
And now, God has miraculously given
His Son, Jesus, to you.
Mercy Me!

Yep, that's it, isn't it?
God's Mercy bestowed on me ...
and God's Mercy miraculously bestowed on you.
Hallelujah! What a Saviour!
Thank You, LORD

"The Lord liveth!
And Blessed be my Rock;
and let The God of my Salvation
be exalted!"

(PSALM 18:46).

OLE SLEWFOOT

MOLLY MCCOY

OLE SLEWFOOT

OLE SLEWFOOT

Is he trackin' YOU down?